Bisclavret and Melion

Two Medieval Werewolf Tales with Original Texts, Translations, and Word Lists

Translated by
Matthew Leigh Embleton

Copyright ©2025 Matthew Leigh Embleton. All rights reserved.

Bisclavret and Melion

Bisclavret by Marie de France 4
Melion by Anonymous 21
Word List *(Old French to English)* 49
Word List *(English to Old French)* 75

Cover: Old French text over an outline of France. Author's design.

The original Old French texts are in the public domain.
These translations ©2021 Matthew Leigh Embleton
©2025 Matthew Leigh Embleton (This Edition)

Acknowledgments

I have long been fascinated by languages and history, and I am very grateful to the special people in my life who have supported and encouraged me in my work. Thank you for believing in me. You know who you are.

Introduction

Bisclavret was written by Marie de France between 1160 and 1175, while Melion was written by an unknown or anonymous writer between 1190 and 1204. While they are several decades apart, they have a number of similarities.

This has led some people to believe that they could in fact originate from the same story, or perhaps they are both inventions drawing on the same source of icons and motifs found in the folklore, myth, and legends of the time.

They are both written in Old French, Bisclavret is in 'Anglo-Norman', whereas Melion is in the 'Picard dialect', both of which are part of the 'Langues d'oïl' dialect continuum of Gallo-Romance languages. Old French is the result of a gradual separation from Vulgar Latin and Common Romance, coming into contact with influences from Gaulish (Continental Celtic), and Frankish (Germanic).

The text is presented in the original Old French, with a literal word-for-word line-by-line translation, and a Modern English translation, all side-by-side. In this way, it is possible to see and feel how Old French worked and how it has evolved.

Also included is a word list with 2,055 Old French words translated in to English, and 1,857 English words translated into Old French.

This book is designed to be of use and interest to anyone with a passion for the Old French language, French history, or languages and history in general.

Marie de France - Bisclavret

Bisclavret

	Old French	Literal	English
1	*Quant des lais faire m'entremet,*	When of-them lays do I-begin,	When I begin (to compose) lays,
2	*ne vueil ubliër Bisclavret.*	not I-wish forget Bisclavret.	I do not wish to forget Bisclavret.
3	*Bisclavret a nun en Bretan,*	Bisclavret has the-name in Breton,	His name is Bisclavret in Breton,
4	*Garulf l'apelent li Norman.*	Garulf they-call the Normans.	The Normans call him Garulf.
5	*Jadis le poeit hum oïr*	Days-passed one could him hear	In days passed one could hear him,
6	*e sovent suleit avenir,*	and time-to-time used frequently,	and this used to happen frequently,
7	*hume plusur garulf devindrent*	man many Garulf became	many a man became a werewolf
8	*e es boscages maisun tindrent.*	and in-those woods house had.	and made his house in the woods.
9	*Garulf, ceo est beste salvage;*	Garulf, behold-this is beast savage;	Werewolf, that is a wild animal;
10	*tant cum il est en cele rage,*	as-much with it is in this rage,	as long as he is in this rage,
11	*humes devure, grant mal fait;*	men devours, great harm does;	He devours men, and does great harm;
12	*es granz forez converse e vait.*	in-those grand forests about and goes.	In the grand forests he goes about.
13	*Cest afaire les ore ester;*	This matter let now stand;	This matter now I let be;
14	*del Bisclavret vus vueil cunter.*	of-this Bisclavret you I-want to-recount.	I want to tell you about Bisclavret.
15	*En Bretaigne maneit uns ber,*	In Brittany lived one baron,	In Brittany there lived a baron,
16	*merveille l'ai oï loër.*	marvellously of-him I-hear praise.	of whom I hear marvellous praise.
17	*Beals chevaliers e bons esteit*	Handsome knight and good he-was	A handsome and good knight he was,
18	*e noblement se cunteneit.*	and nobly he led-himself.	And nobly he led himself.

Marie de France - Bisclavret

	Old French	Literal	English
19	*De sun seignur esteit privez*	Of his lord he-was close	Of his lord he was a close friend,
20	*e de tuz ses veisins amez.*	and of all his neighbours loved.	and by all his neighbours he was loved.
21	*Femme ot espuse mult vaillant*	Woman had wife much valiant	He had a woman as his wife who was much valiant,
22	*e ki mult faiseit bel semblant.*	and of much made beautiful appearance.	and who was beautiful in appearance.
23	*Il amot li e ele lui;*	He loved her and she him;	He loved her, and she loved him;
24	*mes d'une chose ert grant ennui,*	but of-one thing was great grief,	but one thing caused her great grief,
25	*qu'en la semeine le perdeit*	that-in the week him lost	that in the week she lost him,
26	*treis jurs entiers qu'el ne saveit*	three days entire with not knowing	for three days without knowing,
27	*que deveneit ne u alout,*	what became nor where went,	what became of him nor where he went,
28	*ne nuls des soens nïent n'en sout.*	nor none of his nothing about knew.	and none of his people knew about it.
29	*Une feiz esteit repairiez*	One time was-he returned	Once he returned
30	*a sa maisun joius e liez;*	to his home joyous and happy;	to his home joyous and happy;
31	*demandé li a e enquis.*	asked she to and inquired.	she asked and inquired.
32	*Sire', fait el, bealz, dulz amis,*	'My-lord', said she, 'gentle, sweet friend,	'My lord', she said, 'gentle and sweet friend,
33	*une chose vus demandasse*	one thing I-wish to-ask	one thing I wish to ask you
34	*mult volentiers, se jeo osasse;*	much willing, if I dare;	very much, if I dare;
35	*mes jeo criem tant vostre curut*	but I fear so-much your anger	but I fear your anger so much
36	*que nule rien tant ne redut'.*	that any nothing as-much nor dread'.	that there is nothing I dread so much'.
37	*Quant il l'oï, si l'acola,*	When he that-heard, so he-embraced,	When he heard that, he embraced her,

Marie de France - Bisclavret

	Old French	Literal	English
38	vers lui la traist, si la baisa.	to him her drew-close, so her kissed.	drew her close to him, and kissed her.
39	Dame', fait il, or demandez!	'Madam', said he, 'just ask!	'Madam', he said, 'just ask!
40	Ja cele chose ne querrez,	Never such thing not ask,	Never such a thing will you ask,
41	se jo la sai, ne la vus die'.	of me that I-know, not the answer you.	of me that if I know, I will not answer you.
42	Par fei', fet ele, or sui guarie!	By faith, said she, 'now I-am relieved!	'By my faith', she said, 'now I am relieved!'
43	Sire, jeo sui en tel esfrei	My-lord, I am in much fear	My lord, I am in such fear,
44	les jurs quant vus partez de mei.	the days when you part from me.	on the days when you take leave of me.
45	El cuer en ai mult grant dolur	In my-heart in have much great pain	In my heart I have such great pain,
46	e de vus perdre tel poür,	and of you loss such horror,	and such horror at the thought of losing you,
47	se jeo nen ai hastif cunfort,	if I do-not have swift comfort,	that if I do not have swift comfort,
48	bien tost en puis aveir la mort.	well quickly and then have of death.	then I may well die soon.
49	Kar me dites u vus alez,	Come me tell where you go,	Come now, tell me where you go,
50	u vus estes e conversez!	where you are and about!	where you are, and where you dwell!
51	Mun esciënt que vus amez,	To-me it-seems that you-have a-love,	It seems to me as though you have a sweetheart,
52	e se si est, vus meserrez'.	and if so are, you misguided'.	and if so, you are misguided'.
53	Dame', fet il, pur deu merci!	'Madam', said he, by god's mercy!	'Madam', he said, 'by god's mercy!
54	Mals m'en vendra, se jol vus di;	Bad to-me comes, if I you tell;	Bad will come to me, if I tell you;
55	kar de m'amur vus partirai	therefore of my-love yours will-part	therefore my love will part,
56	e mei meïsmes en perdrai'.	and me myself then destroy.	and then me myself will be destroyed.

Marie de France - Bisclavret

	Old French	Literal	English
57	Quant la dame l'a entendu,	When the lady this heard,	When the lady heard this,
58	ne l'a nïent en gab tenu.	nor that nothing in jest beheld.	she knew that it was not in jest.
59	Suventes feiz li demanda.	Repeatedly put she questions.	Repeatedly she asked him questions.
60	Tant le blandi e losenja	So-much him cajoled and praised	So she flattered and praised him,
61	que s'aventure li cunta;	that his-adventure he recounted;	that he told her of his adventure;
62	nule chose ne li cela.	any thing not was concealed.	and nothing did he conceal from her.
63	Dame, jeo deviene bisclavret.	Madam, I become Bisclavret.	Madam, I become a werewolf.
64	En cele grant forest me met	In that great forest I go	In that great forest I go,
65	al plus espés de la gualdine,	to most thick of the forest,	to the thickest part of the woods,
66	s'i vif de preie e de ravine'.	thus live by plunder and of theft.	and there I live by plunder and theft.
67	Quant il li aveit tut cunté,	When he her had all recounted,	When he had recounted everything to her,
68	enquis li a e demandé	queried she and of asked	she queried him and asked him
69	s'il se despueille u vet vestuz.	whether he unclothed or goes dressed.	whether he went clothed or unclothed.
70	Dame', fet il, jeo vois tuz nuz'.	Madam', said he, 'I go totally nude'.	Madam', he said, 'I go totally naked'.
71	Di mei pur deu u sunt voz dras!'	'Tell me by god where are your clothes!'	'Tell me by god where are your clothes!'
72	Dame, ceo ne dirai jeo pas;	'Madam, this not will-tell I not;	'Madam, this I do not want to tell you;
73	kar se jes eüsse perduz	because if I were to-lose	because if I were to lose them,
74	e de ceo fusse aparceüz,	and of that had-been aware,	and if I become aware (of losing them),
75	bisclavret sereie a tuz jurs.	Bisclavret I-would-be of all days.	I would be a werewolf for all days.
76	Ja nen avreie mes sucurs,	I not could me help,	No help could ever again avail me,
77	desi qu'il me fussent rendu.	until which to-me would-be returned.	until they would be returned to me.

Marie de France - Bisclavret

	Old French	Literal	English
78	Pur ceo ne vueil qu'il seit seü'.	Therefore this not want which to-be known.	Therefore that is why I do not wish it to be known.
79	Sire', la dame li respunt,	'My-lord', the woman to-him responded,	'My lord', the woman responded to him,
80	jeo vus eim plus que tut le mund.	'I you love more than all the world.	'I love you more than all the world.
81	Nel me devez niënt celer	Not me should nothing conceal	Nothing should you conceal from me,
82	ne mei de nule rien duter;	nor mine of any nothing doubt;	Nor doubt my understanding of anything;
83	ne semblereit pas amistié,	not would-look-like not friendship,	that would not look like friendship,
84	Qu'ai jeo forfait, pur quel pechié	what-have I committed, by what sin	what have I committed, and by what sin
85	me dutez vus de nule rien?	me doubt you of not nothing?	that you doubt me not of nothing?
86	Dites le mei! Si ferez bien'.	Tell it to-me! So will-do well.	Tell me, so you will do well.
87	Tant l'anguissa, tant le suzprist,	So anguish, such he under-pressed,	Such anguish, he was pressed,
88	ne pout el faire, si li dist.	naught could he do, but her tell.	there was naught he could do but tell her.
89	Dame', fet il, de lez cel bois,	'Madam', said he, 'of near the forest,	Madam', he said, 'near the forest,
90	lez le chemin par unt jeo vois,	near the path by then I go,	near the path I go by,
91	une viez chapele i estait,	an old chapel is standing,	there stands an old chapel,
92	ki meinte feiz grant bien me fait.	which many times great good me has-done.	which many times has done me well.
93	La est la piere cruese e lee	There is the stone hollow and wide	There is a hollow and wide stone
94	suz un buissun, dedenz cavee.	under a bush, inside dug-out.	under a bush, inside a dug-out.
95	Mes dras i met suz le buissun,	My clothes I put under the bush,	I put my clothes under the bush,
96	tant que jeo revienc a maisun'.	until that I return to home.	until I return home.

Marie de France - Bisclavret

	Old French	Literal	English
97	La dame oï cele merveille,	The lady heard this marvel,	The lady heard this marvel,
98	de poür fu tute vermeille.	with fear became all crimson.	and became crimson with fear.
99	De l'aventure s'esfrea.	By the-event she-was-terrified.	By the event she was terrified.
100	En maint endreit se purpensa	In many ways she purposed	In many ways she thought,
101	cum ele s'en peüst partir;	how she if could part-with;	how she could part with him;
102	ne voleit mes lez lui gisir.	no-longer wanted with near him to-lie.	no longer did she want to lie near him.
103	Un chevalier de la cuntree,	A knight from the country,	A knight from the country,
104	ki lungement l'aveit amee	which long her-had loved	Who had long loved her
105	e mult preiee e mult requise	and much courted and much desired	and much courted and desired her
106	e mult duné en sun servise,	and much dedicated to her service,	and was much dedicated to her service,
107	(ele ne l'aveit unc amé	(she not him-had never loved	(she had never loved him,
108	ne de s'amur aseüré),	nor of love assured),	nor assured him of her love),
109	celui manda par sun message,	for-him sent-for by a message,	she sent for him by message,
110	si li descovri sun curage.	and to-him revealed her heart.	and revealed her sentiments to him.
111	Amis', fet ele, seiez liez!	'Friend', said she, 'be happy!	Friend', she said, 'be happy!
112	Ceo dunt vus estes travailliez	That which you are striving	That what you have been striving for
113	vus otrei jeo senz nul respit;	you grant I without any delay;	I grant you without any delay;
114	ja n'i avrez nul cuntredit.	never none will have any opposition.	you will never have any opposition.
115	M'amur e mun cors vus otrei:	my-love and my body yours grant:	My love and my body I grant you:

Marie de France - Bisclavret

	Old French	Literal	English
116	*vostre drue faites de mei!'*	your mistress make of me!'	make me your mistress!'
117	*Cil l'en mercie bonement*	This-he her thanks very-well	For this he thanks her very well
118	*e la fiance de li prent,*	and her promise of he receives,	and he receives her promise,
119	*e el le met a sairement.*	and she him puts under oath.	and she puts him under oath.
120	*Puis li cunta cumfaitement*	Then she recounted in-such-way	Then she told him which way
121	*sis sire ala e qu'il devint.*	her husband went and what became.	her husband went and what became of him.
122	*Tute la veie que il tint*	All the way that he travelled	The whole way that he travelled
123	*vers la forest li enseigna;*	to the forest she indicated;	to the forest she indicated;
124	*pur sa despueille l'enveia.*	for his clothes she-sent-for.	she sent him for her husband's clothes.
125	*Issi fu Bisclavret traïz*	Thus was Bisclavret betrayed	Thus was Bisclavret betrayed
126	*e par sa femme mal bailliz.*	and by this woman badly treated.	and treated badly by this woman.
127	*Pur ceo qu'um le perdeit sovent,*	Because that of-him one missed frequently,	Because he was frequently absent,
128	*quidouent tuit comunalment*	thought-they all together	they all thought together,
129	*que dunc s'en fust del tut alez.*	that so it was of all gone.	that he had gone for good.
130	*Asez fu quis e demandez:*	Much was he of sought-for:	Much was he sought and hunted for:
131	*mes n'en porent mie trover,*	but not could-they not-at-all find,	But they could not at all find him,
132	*si lur estut laissier ester.*	so let stand left was.	and so it was let be.
133	*La dame a cil dunc espusee,*	The woman then him so married,	The woman then married the one,
134	*que lungement aveit amee.*	who long had loved.	who had long lover her.

Marie de France - Bisclavret

	Old French	Literal	English
135	*Issi remest un an entier,*	So remained one year entire,	So remained a whole year,
136	*tant que li reis ala chacier.*	until that the king of-the hunt.	until the king joined the hunt.
137	*A la forest ala tut dreit*	To the forest of all straight	to the forest his way led straight
138	*la u li Bisclavret esteit.*	there where he Bisclavret stayed.	there where the were Bisclavret stayed.
139	*Quant li chien furent descuplé,*	When the dogs were released,	When the dogs were released,
140	*le Bisclavret unt encuntré.*	the Bisclavret they encountered.	they encountered Bisclavret.
141	*A lui cururent tutejur*	Of him chased all-the-day	They chased him all day
142	*e li chien e li veneür,*	and the dogs and the hunters,	and the dogs and hunters,
143	*tant que pur poi ne l'ourent pris*	until which all but not caught prize	all but caught him
144	*e tut deciré e mal mis.*	and all tear and badly treated.	and all but tore and ripped him.
145	*Des que il a le rei choisi,*	Of when he of the king saw,	And when he saw the king,
146	*vers lui curut querre merci.*	went he running asking-for mercy.	He went running asking for mercy.
147	*Il l'aveit pris par sun estrié,*	He had seized by his stirrup,	He seized him by his stirrup,
148	*la jambe li baise e le pié.*	his leg he kisses and his feet.	kissed his legs and feet.
149	*Li reis le vit, grant poür a;*	The king him saw, great fear had;	When the king saw him, he had great fear;
150	*ses cumpaignuns tuz apela.*	his companions all he-called.	he called all his companions.
151	*Seignur', fet il, avant venez!*	'Sires', said he, 'forward come!	'Sires', he said, 'come forward!
152	*Iceste merveille esguardez,*	This marvel look-at,	Look at this marvel,
153	*cum ceste beste s'umilie!*	how this beast is-humbled!	how the beast is humbled!

Marie de France - Bisclavret

	Old French	Literal	English
154	*Ele a sen d'ume, merci crie.*	He has sense of-a-man, mercy asks-for.	He has the sense of a man, who asks for mercy.
155	*Chaciez mei tuz cez chiens ariere,*	Chase from-me all these dogs back,	Chase from me all these dogs back,
156	*si guardez que hum ne la fiere!*	and take-care that he not is hit!	and take care that he is not hit!.
157	*Ceste beste a entente e sen.*	This beast has reason and sense.	This beast has reason and sense.
158	*Espleitiez vus! Alum nus en!*	Hurry you! Let-us we go!	Hurry! Let us all go!
159	*A la beste durrai ma pes:*	To the beast grant my peace:	To the beast grant my peace:
160	*kar jeo ne chacerai hui mes'.*	because I not will-hunt this-day furthermore.	Because from this day I do not wish to hunt any more.
161	*Li reis s'en est turnez a tant.*	The king then was returned at such-time.	The king then returned after a time.
162	*Li Bisclavret le vet siwant;*	The Bisclavret him there followed;	The Bisclavret followed him there;
163	*mult se tint pres, n'en volt partir,*	much he travels close, nor wants to-part,	he travels close to him, not wanting to leave him,
164	*il n'a cure de lui guerpir,*	he not-has care of him abandoning,	taking care not to abandon him,
165	*Li reis l'en meine en sun chastel.*	The king him takes to his castle.	The king takes him to his castle.
166	*Mult en fu liez, mult li est bel,*	Very he is happy, much he is well,	He is very happy, and very much well,
167	*kar unkes mes tel n'ot veü;*	because never he has before seen;	because he has never seen before;
168	*a grant merveille l'ot tenu*	a great wonder before beheld	a great wonder before beheld
169	*e mult le tint a grant chierté.*	and much him held of great fondness.	and he held him in great fondness.
170	*A tuz les suens a comandé*	Of all his people he commanded	Of all his people he commanded
171	*que sur s'amur le guardent bien*	for sure for-the-love-of him guard well	for the king's sake to guard him well
172	*e ne li mesfacent de rien,*	and not him harm of any,	and cause him no harm,

Marie de France - Bisclavret

	Old French	Literal	English
173	*ne par nul d'els ne seit feruz;*	nor by anyone be he to-be beaten;	nor be beaten by anyone;
174	*bien seit abevrez e peüz.*	well to-be drink and food.	to be given drink and food.
175	*Cil le guarderent volentiers*	They him guarded gladly	They guarded him gladly.
176	*tuz jurs entre les chevaliers,*	all days among the knights,	All days he was among the knights,
177	*e pres del rei s'alout culchier.*	and close to the-king next-to slept.	And next to the king he slept.
178	*N'i a celui ki ne l'ait chier;*	No-one is who-him that not has love;	There is no one who does not love him;
179	*tant esteit frans e de bon aire:*	so noble engaging and of good appearance:	so noble engaging and of good appearance:
180	*unkes ne volt a rien mesfaire.*	never nor willed of anything misdeed.	never did he wish to do anything wrong.
181	*U que li reis deüst errer,*	Where which the king had to-go,	Where the king had to go,
182	*il n'out cure de desevrer;*	he not-had care of to-separate;	he did not care to separate from him;
183	*ensemble od lui tuz jurs alout,*	with among him all days he-went,	with him he always went,
184	*bien s'aparceit que il l'amout.*	well he-perceived that he him-loved.	and he perceived well that he loved him.
185	*Oëz aprés cument avint!*	Hear after what happened!	Hear what happened after!
186	*A une curt que li reis tint*	At a court which the king held	At a court which the king held
187	*tuz les baruns aveit mandez,*	all the barons he-had ordered,	he had ordered all the barons,
188	*cels ki furent de ses chasez,*	those which he-had of full fief,	those which he had fiefdom over,
189	*pur aidier sa feste a tenir*	for to-help his party to have	to contribute to his party

Marie de France - Bisclavret

	Old French	Literal	English
190	e lui plus bel faire servir.	and him more well made served.	and serve him more graciously.
191	Li chevaliers i est alez,	The knight he is gone,	The knight he has gone,
192	richement e bien aturnez,	richly and well dressed,	richly and well dressed,
193	ki la femme Bisclavret ot.	who had the-wife Bisclavret of.	who had the wife of Bisclavret.
194	Il ne saveit ne ne quidot	He not knew not no thought	He did not know and did not think
195	qu'il le deüst trover si pres.	which-that he would find so close.	that he would find him so close.
196	Si tost cum il vint al palais	As soon as he came to the-palace	As soon as he came to the palace
197	e li Bisclavret l'aperceut,	and him Bisclavret noticed,	and Bisclavret noticed him,
198	de plein eslais vers lui curut:	of full run towards him ran:	at full speed he ran towards him:
199	as denz le prist, vers lui le trait.	in teeth his seized, towards him he draws.	in his teeth he seized him, toward him he draws him.
200	Ja li eüst mult grant laid fait,	Now he would-have much great harm done,	Now he would have done great harm,
201	ne fust li reis ki l'apela,	not had the king him called,	If the king had not called him,
202	d'une verge le manaça.	with-a stick him threatened.	and threatened him with a stick.
203	Dous feiz le volt mordre le jur.	Two times he wanted to-bite him that-day.	Twice that day he wanted to bite him.
204	Mult s'esmerveillent li plusur;	Most astonished him more;	Most people were more astonished;
205	kar unkes tel semblant ne fist	because never had appeared not been-so	because he had never appeared like this
206	vers nul hume que il veïst.	toward any man whom he saw.	toward any man whom he saw.
207	Ceo diënt tuit par la maisun	Everyone said all by the house	Everyone in the house said
208	qu'il nel fet mie senz raisun,	that not act not-at-all without reason,	that he did not act without a reason,

Marie de France - Bisclavret

	Old French	Literal	English
209	*mesfait li a, coment que seit,*	mistreatment he had, somehow which been,	some injury or mistreatment had somehow been done to him,
210	*kar volentiers se vengereit.*	because he-wanted to avenge-himself.	because he wanted to avenge himself.
211	*A cele feiz remest issi,*	At that-time nothing more happened,	At that time nothing more happened,
212	*tant que la feste departi;*	until that the party departed;	until the party had departed;
213	*e li barun unt pris cungié,*	and the barons they took leave,	and the barons took leave,
214	*a lur maisun sunt repairié.*	to their homes they went.	and went to their homes.
215	*Alez s'en est li chevaliers,*	Gone it is the knight,	Gone is the knight,
216	*mien esciënt tut as premiers,*	among it-seems all the first,	among the first it seems,
217	*que li Bisclavret asailli;*	which the Bisclavret assailed;	which the Bisclavret had attacked;
218	*n'est merveille s'il le haï.*	not-is wonder if-him he hated.	no wonder if he hated him.
219	*Ne fu puis guaires lungement,*	Not happened since much long-after,	It happened not long after this,
220	*(ceo m'est a vis, si cum j'entent),*	(such is as so, if with I-understand),	(such as it is, if I understand),
221	*qu'a la forest ala li reis,*	that to-the forest went the king,	that the king went to the forest,
222	*ki tant fu sages e curteis,*	who was so understanding and courteous,	who was so understanding and courteous,
223	*u li Bisclavret fu trovez;*	where the Bisclavret was found;	to where the Bisclavret was found;
224	*e il i est od lui alez.*	and he with was among him went.	and there with him he went.
225	*La nuit quant il s'en repaira,*	The night when he was returned,	In the night when he came back,
226	*en la cuntree herberja.*	in the country he-stayed.	in the country he stayed.
227	*La femme Bisclavret le sot.*	The woman Bisclavret the found-out.	The wife of Bisclavret found out.

Marie de France - Bisclavret

	Old French	Literal	English
228	*Avenantment s'apareillot.*	Attractively she-dressed.	Attractively she dressed.
229	*Al demain vait al rei parler,*	In the-morning went to-the king to-talk-with,	In the morning she went to see the king,
230	*riche present li fait porter.*	expensive present she does bring.	an expensive gift she brings him.
231	*Quant Bisclavret la veit venir,*	When Bisclavret her sees coming,	When Bisclavret sees her coming,
232	*nuls huem nel poeit retenir:*	none man not can retain-him:	no man can hold him back:
233	*vers li curut cum enragiez.*	towards her he-runs as-though enraged.	towards her he runs as though enraged.
234	*Oëz cum il s'est bien vengiez!*	Listen how he is well avenged!	Listen to how he is well avenged!
235	*Le nes li esracha del vis.*	Her nose he snatched from face.	Her nose he snatched from her face.
236	*Que li peüst il faire pis?*	What he worse he done could-have?	What worse could he have done?
237	*De tutes parz l'unt manacié;*	From all sides they threatened;	From all sides they threatened him;
238	*ja l'eüssent tut depescié,*	indeed they-would-have all dismembered,	indeed they would have dismembered him,
239	*quant uns sages huem dist al rei:*	when one wise man said to the-king:	when one wise man said to the king:
240	*Sire', fet il, entent a mei!*	'Sire', said he, 'listen to me!	Sire', he said, 'listen to me!'
241	*Ceste beste a esté od vus;*	This beast has been with you;	This beast has been with you;
242	*n'i a ore celui de nus*	none is presently that-one of us	none of us who are present
243	*ki ne l'ait veü lungement*	who not has known-him long	have not known him long
244	*e pres de lui alé sovent.*	and close of him gone often.	and been close with him often.
245	*Unkes mes hume ne tucha*	Never more man not harm	Never more did he harm any man
246	*ne felunie ne mustra,*	nor felony none commit,	Nor commit any felony,

Marie de France - Bisclavret

	Old French	Literal	English
247	*fors a la dame qu'ici vei.*	except to the woman who-here you-see.	except in the case of the woman you see here.
248	*Par cele fei que jeo vus dei,*	By that faith that I you owe,	By that faith I owe you,
249	*alkun curuz a il vers li*	some anger has he against her	he has some anger against her
250	*e vers sun seignur altresi.*	and against her husband also.	and against her husband also.
251	*Ceo est la femme al chevalier*	This is the wife of the-knight	This is the wife of the knight
252	*que tant suliëz aveir chier,*	whom that previously have loved,	whom you used to love,
253	*ki lung tens a esté perduz,*	who long held that was lost,	who for such a long time was lost,
254	*ne seümes qu'est devenuz.*	nor knew what became-of.	nor known what had become of him.
255	*Kar metez la dame en destreit,*	Therefore place the woman with difficulty,	Therefore force that woman's hand,
256	*s'alcune chose vus direit,*	if-some thing you tells,	so that she might tell you something,
257	*pur quei ceste beste la het.*	for what this beast her hates.	why this beast hates her.
258	*Faites li dire s'el le set!*	Makes her say if-she this knows!	Make her say if she knows why!
259	*Meinte merveille avum veüe*	Many wonders have-we seen	Many wonders we have seen
260	*ki en Bretaigne est avenue'.*	which in Brittany that happened.	which in Brittany that happened.
261	*Li reis a sun cunseil creü.*	The king of his counsel believed.	The king believed his counsel.
262	*Le chevalier a retenu;*	The knight was retained;	The knight was retained;
263	*de l'altre part la dame a prise*	of the-other part the woman was taken-aside	on the other hand, the woman was taken aside
264	*e en mult grant destresce mise.*	and then much great distress questioned.	and then distressed with many questions.
265	*Tant par destresce e par poür*	As-much by distress and by fear	As much by distress and by fear

Marie de France - Bisclavret

	Old French	Literal	English
266	tut li cunta de sun seignur,	all she recounted of her husband,	she recounted all of her husband,
267	coment ele l'aveit traï	how she had betrayed	how she had betrayed him
268	e sa despueille li toli,	and how clothes his taken-away,	and how his clothes had been taken away,
269	l'aventure qu'il li cunta,	the-adventure which-of she recounted,	she told him of the adventure,
270	e que devint e u ala;	and what became and where he-went;	and what became of him and where he went;
271	puis que ses dras li ot toluz,	after that his clothes she away took,	after she took his clothes away,
272	ne fu en sun païs veüz;	not was he in country seen;	he was no longer seen in the country;
273	tresbien quidot e bien creeit	very-well thought that well believed	she thought and very well believed
274	que la beste Bisclavret seit.	that the beast Bisclavret to-be.	that the beast was Bisclavret.
275	Li reis demande sa despueille.	The king asked for the-clothing.	The king asks for the clothing.
276	U bel li seit u pas nel vueille,	Whether well he to-be or not nor want,	Whether he wants it or not,
277	ariere la fet aporter,	to-him it had brought,	to him it was brought,
278	al Bisclavret la fist doner.	to Bisclavret the has-it given.	to Bisclavret has it given.
279	Quant il l'orent devant lui mise,	When they had before him set,	When they put it before him,
280	ne s'en prist guarde en nule guise.	not did-he pay attention in no way.	he did not pay attention in any way.
281	Li prozdum le rei apela,	The worthy-man who the-king addressed,	The worthy man who addressed the king,
282	cil ki primes le cunseilla.	he who first him counselled.	he who first advised him.
283	Sire, ne faites mie bien!	'Sire, not done not-at-all well!	Sire, it is not done well at all!'
284	Cist nel fereit pur nule rien,	The-last among doing by any nothing,	The last thing he will do,
285	que devant vus ses dras reveste	that before your sight clothes re-dress	is re-dress before your sight
286	ne mut la semblance de beste.	nor change his appearance from the-beast.	nor change his appearance from the beast.

Marie de France - Bisclavret

	Old French	Literal	English
287	Ne savez mie que ceo munte.	You know not that this very-important.	You do not know that this is very important.
288	Mult durement en a grant hunte.	Very hard is a great shame.	Very hard is the great shame.
289	En tes chambres le fai mener	In your rooms him let be-taken	Let him be taken to your rooms,
290	e la despueille od lui porter;	and there clothes with him brought;	And have clothes brought to him;
291	une grant piece l'i laissuns.	a great part him let-us-leave.	And let us leave him for a time.
292	S'il devient huem, bien le verruns'.	if-he becomes a-man, well this we-will-see.	Whether he becomes a man, we will see.
293	Li reis meïsmes l'en mena	The king himself he there took	The king himself took him there
294	e tuz les hus sur lui ferma.	and all the doors behind him closed.	and all the doors behind him closed.
295	Al chief de piece i est alez;	At the-end of the-time there he went;	At the end of a time he went there;
296	dous baruns a od lui menez.	two barons that with him took.	he took two barons with him.
297	En la chambre entrerent tuit trei.	Unto the room entered all three.	All three entered the room.
298	Sur le demeine lit al rei	On his own bed the king's	On the king's own bed
299	truevent dormant le chevalier.	they-find sleeping the knight.	they find the knight sleeping.
300	Li reis le curut enbracier;	The king him ran to-embrace;	The king ran to embrace him;
301	plus de cent feiz l'acole e baise.	more than a-hundred times embraces and kisses.	more than a hundred times, he embraces and kisses him.
302	Si tost cum il pot aveir aise,	As soon as he could have facility,	As soon as he had the opportunity,
303	Tute sa terre li rendi,	All his land to-him returned,	He returned all his land to him,
304	plus li duna que jeo ne di.	more him gave than I can tell.	and gave him more than I can tell.
305	La femme a del païs ostee	The woman of from the-country banned	The woman was banned from the country

Marie de France - Bisclavret

	Old French	Literal	English
306	e chaciee de la cuntree.	and chased out-of the country.	and chased out of the country.
307	Cil s'en ala ensemble od li,	The-one who along together with her,	The one who went with her,
308	pur qui sun seignur ot traï.	for whom her husband had betrayed.	for whom she had betrayed her husband.
309	Enfanz en a asez eüz,	Children with of many they-had,	They had many children,
310	puis unt esté bien cuneüz	could they be well known	they were well known
311	e del semblant e del visage:	by of appearance and of face:	by their appearance and by their faces:
312	plusurs des femmes del lignage,	many of women of lineage,	many women of their lineage,
313	c'est veritez, senz nes sunt nees	it-is true, without noses they-were born	it is true, were born with out noses
314	e si viveient esnasees.	and thus they-live noselessly.	and so they lived noselessly.
315	L'aventure qu'avez oïe	The-story which you-heard	The story which you heard
316	veraie fu, n'en dutez mie.	true was, do-not doubt not-at-all.	was true, do not doubt at all.
317	De Bisclavret fu fez li lais	Of Bisclavret was composed this lay	This lay was composed of Bisclavret
318	pur remembrance a tuz dis mais.	for remembrance of all tell more.	for remembrance of all more to tell.

Anonymous - Melion

Melion

	Old French	Literal	English
1	*Al tans que rois Artus regnoit -*	At time when king Arthur reigned	At the time when King Arthur reigned
2	*Cil ki les terres conqueroit,*	He who the lands conquered,	He who conquered lands
3	*Et qui dona les riches dons*	And who gave the rich gifts	And who gave rich gifts
4	*As chevaliers et as barons -*	The knights and the barons	To knights and to barons
5	*Avoit od lui .I. bacheler;*	Had with him one knight;	He had with him a knight;
6	*Melïon l'ai oï nomer.*	Melion I have heard called.	I have heard him called Melion.
7	*Molt par estoit cortois et prous*	Very by was courtly and noble	He was very courtly and noble,
8	*Et amer se faisoit a tos.*	And loved he was-made by all.	And he made himself beloved by all.
9	*Molt ert de grant chevalerie*	Many was of great knights	He was in a great band of knights
10	*Et de cortoise compaignie.*	And of courtly company.	And of courtly company.
11	*Li rois ot molt riche maisnie;*	The king had very rich household;	The king kept a very rich household;
12	*Par tot le mont estoit proisie*	By all the world was praised	It was praised by all the world
13	*De cortoisie et de proece*	Of courtesy and of prowess	For its courtesy and prowess
14	*Et de bonté et de largece.*	And of excellence and of largesse.	And its excellence and generosity.
15	*A icel jor lor veu faisoient,*	And one day their vows they-were-making,	One day they were making their vows
16	*Et sachiés bien k'il le gardoient.*	And be-sure well that they kept.	And you may be very sure that they kept them.
17	*Cil Melïons .I. en voa*	This Melion one of vow	This Melion made one vow
18	*Que a grant mal li atorna:*	Which to great harm to-him returned:	Which returned on him great harm:
19	*Il dist ja n'ameroit pucele,*	He said never enamoured maiden,	He said he would never love a maiden,
20	*Que tant seroit gentil ne bele,*	Who so-much was noble or beautiful,	No matter how noble or beautiful,
21	*Que nul autre home eüst amé,*	Who any other man would-have loved,	Who had loved any other man

Anonymous - Melion

	Old French	Literal	English
22	Ne que de nul eüst parlé.	Or who of any would-have spoken.	Or even had spoken of any.
23	Une grant piece fu ensi:	A great time happened so-as-this:	For a great time matters stood like this:
24	Cil ki le veu orent oï	They who this vow prayed heard	Those who had heard this vow
25	En pluisors lieus le recorderent	Then many places this repeated	Repeated it in many places
26	Et as puceles le conterent;	And the maidens they heard;	And the maidens they heard;
27	Et qant les puceles l'oïrent	And when the maidens heard	And when the maidens heard
28	Molt durement l'en enhaïrent.	Much greatly him they-hated.	They hated him for it very much.
29	Celes ki es canbres estoient	Those who in-those chambers they-were	Those who were ladies-in-waiting
30	Et ki la roïne servoient,	And who the queen they-served,	And who served the queen,
31	Dont il en i ot plus de cent,	Of-whom they of there had more than a-hundred,	Of whom there were more than a hundred,
32	En ont tenu .I. parlement:	On-which they beheld a meeting:	Held a meeting about it:
33	Dïent jamais ne l'ameront,	They-said never not him-they-would-love,	They said they would never love him
34	N'encontre lui ne parleront;	nor-meet him not they-speak;	Nor speak to him;
35	Dame nel voloit regarder,	Lady nor wished-to look-at-him,	No lady wished to look at him,
36	Ne pucelë a lui parler.	Nor maiden to him speak.	Nor any maiden to speak to him.
37	Qant Melïon ice oï,	When Melion this heard,	When Melion heard this,
38	Molt durement s'en asopli;	Very hard was-he downcast;	He was very downcast;
39	Ne voloit mais querre aventure,	Not he-wished more to-seek adventure,	He no longer wished to seek adventure
40	Ne d'armes porter n'avoit cure.	Nor of-arms to-bear not-having a-care.	Nor did he care to bear arms.
41	Molt fu dolans, molt asopli,	Much became sorrow, much downcast,	He was sorrowful, very unhappy,
42	Et de son pris alques perdi.	And of his esteem somewhat lost.	And he lost his esteem somewhat.
43	Li rois le sot, molt l'en pesa,	This the-king he found-out, much him weighed-upon,	The king found this out, it weighed very heavily on him;

Anonymous - Melion

	Old French	Literal	English
44	Mander le fist, a lui parla.	Commanded he be, to him to-speak.	He had Melion sent for and spoke
45	'Melïons', fait li rois Artus,	Melion', said he king Arthur,	Melion', said King Arthur,
46	'Tes grans sens qu'est il devenus,	'Your great sense what has become,	What has become of your great sense,
47	Ton pris et ta chevalerie?	Your esteem and your chivalry?	Your esteem and your chivalry?
48	Di que tu as, nel celes mie.	Say what you have, nor hide none-at-all.	Say what's wrong, hide none of it.
49	Se tu veus terre ne manoir,	If you want land or a-manor,	If you want land or a manor,
50	N'autre cose que puisse avoir,	or-other things which I-may have,	Or any other thing I may have,
51	Se il est en ma roiauté,	If it is in my realm,	If it is in my realm
52	Tu l'avras a ta volenté.	You shall-have as your wish.	You shall have it as you wish.
53	Volentiers te rehaiteroie',	Willingly you comfort,	I would willingly comfort you',
54	Ce dist li rois, 'se jo pooie.	This said the king, 'if I could.	Said the king, 'if I could.
55	Un castel ai sor cele mer;	A castle have on the sea;	I have a castle on the coast;
56	En tot cest siecle n'a itel.	In all this age not-has-been the-same.	There's not such a one in this age.
57	Beax est de bois et de riviere	Beautiful it-is of forests and of rivers	It has beautiful woods, rivers
58	Et de forest que molt as chiere.	And of forest that much you dearly-love.	And forests, that you love so much.
59	Cel te donrai por rehaitier,	This you i-will-give for comfort,	I shall give you this to comfort you;
60	Bien t'i porras esbanoier.'	Well you may enjoy'.	You can enjoy yourself there very well'.
61	Li rois li a en fief doné;	The king him to of-it fief gave;	The king gave it to him in fief;
62	Melïons l'en a mercïé.	Melion him he thanked.	Melion thanked him for it.
63	A son castel en est alé,	To his castel on is going,	He set out for his castle,
64	.C. chevaliers i a mené.	A-hundred knights with he took.	And took a hundred knights there.
65	Li païs bien li conteça	He the-country well him contented	The country pleased him well,

Anonymous - Melion

	Old French	Literal	English
66	Et la forest que molt ama.	And the forest which much he-loved.	And the forest, which he loved very much.
67	Qant il i ot .I. an esté,	When he there away one year had-been,	When he had been there for a year,
68	Molt a le païs enamé,	Much of the country he-loved,	He loved the country greatly,
69	Car ja deduit ne demandast	For already pleasure not asked-for	For there was no pleasure he may ask for
70	Que en la forest ne trovast.	Which in the forest could-not find.	That he could not find in the forest.
71	Un jor estoit alé chacier	One day was going the-hunt	One day Melion went hunting,
72	Melïon et si forestier.	Melion and his foresters.	Melion and his foresters.
73	Od lui furent si veneor,	Among him had his huntsmen,	Among him had his huntsmen,
74	Ki l'amerent de bone amor	Who him-loved of good love	Who loved him truly
75	Car ce estoit lor liges sire;	Because he was their liege sire;	Because he was their liege sire;
76	Totes honors en lui remire.	All honour was him admired.	All honour was reflected in him.
77	Tost orent .I. grant cerf trové,	Quickly had one great stag found,	Soon they found a great stag;
78	Tost l'orent pris et descoplé.	Immediately had took and unleashed.	Quickly they took and unleashed the hounds.
79	En une lande s'aresta	And one land he-stopped	Melion stopped in a heath
80	Por sa meute k'il escouta.	For how might which-he listen.	So he could listen for the pack of hounds.
81	Od lui estoit uns escuiers,	Among, with him, him was one squire,	With him was a squire;
82	En sa main tenoit .II. levriers.	And his hand held two greyhounds.	He was restraining two greyhounds in his hand.
83	En la lande, qu'est verde et bele,	In his heath, which-is green and beautiful,	In this heath, which was green and beautiful,
84	Vit Melïons une pucele	Saw Melion a maiden	Melion saw a maiden
85	Venir sor .I. bel palefroi;	Coming on one beautiful palfrey;	Approaching on a handsome palfrey;
86	Molt erent riche si conroi.	Much were rich of the-trappings.	The trappings were most rich.
87	Un vermeil samit ot vestu,	A vermillion rich-silk had wearing,	She was dressed in vermillion silk

Anonymous - Melion

	Old French	Literal	English
88	*Estoit a las molt bien cosu;*	Was of lace very well sewn;	Which was sewn well with laces;
89	*A son col .I. mantel d'ermine;*	On her shoulders one mantle of-ermine;	Around her shoulders was an ermine
90	*Ainc meillor n'afubla roïne.*	Rather better than-worn a-queen.	No queen ever wore better.
91	*Gent cors et bele espauleüre,*	Beautiful body and elegant shoulders,	A pleasing figure, elegant shoulders
92	*Et blonde la cheveleüre.*	And blonde her hair.	And blonde was her hair.
93	*Petite bouche bien mollee*	Petite mouth well shaped	A nicely shaped petite mouth,
94	*Et comme rose encoloree;*	And as rose coloured;	The colour of a rose;
95	*Les ex ot vairs, clers et rians:*	Her eyes with bright, clear and sparlking:	She had bright eyes, clear and sparkling:
96	*Molt estoit bele en tos samblans.*	Much was beauty in all appearance.	She was very beautiful in her whole appearance.
97	*Seule venoit sans compaignie,*	Alone came without company,	She came alone without company,
98	*Molt par fu gente et escavie.*	Much by was elegant and charming.	And was most elegant and charming.
99	*Melïon contre lui en va;*	Melion to-greet her he went;	Melion went to meet her;
100	*Molt belement le salua.*	Very politely he greeted.	He greeted her very politely.
101	*'Bele', dist il, 'jo vos salu*	'Fair-lady', said he, 'I you greet	Fair lady', he said, 'I greet you
102	*Del glorious, le roi Jesu.*	From glorious, the king Jesus.	From glorious, the king Jesus.
103	*Dites moi dont vos estes nee*	Tell me of-where you are born	Tell me where you were born
104	*Et que ici vos a menee.'*	And what here you has brought'.	And what has brought you here'.
105	*Cele respont: 'Jel vos dirai,*	This responded: 'I-will you tell,	She replied: 'I shall tell you about it,
106	*Que ja de mot n'en mentirai.*	For I of words not-of shall-lie.	I shall not tell you a word of a lie.
107	*Je sui assez de haut parage*	I am rather of high family	I am of very high birth
108	*Et nee de gentil lignage.*	And born of noble lineage.	And born of noble lineage.
109	*D'Yrlande sui a vos venue;*	From-Ireland I-am to you arriving;	I have come to you from Ireland;

Anonymous - Melion

	Old French	Literal	English
110	Sachiés que je sui molt vo drue.	Know-you that I am very-much your mistress.	Know that I am entirely your lover.
111	Onques home fors vos n'amai,	Never man except you have-I-loved,	I have never loved a man other than you
112	Ne jamais plus n'en amerai.	Nor never another not shall-I-love.	Nor shall I ever love another.
113	Forment vos ai oï loer,	Greatly you have-I heard praised,	I have heard you greatly praised,
114	Onques ne voloie altre amer	Never none wished other to-love	I never desired to love any other
115	Fors vos tot seul; ne jamais jor	Except you completely only; nor never a-day	But you alone; never at any time
116	Vers nul autre n'avrai amor.'	To none other shall-I love'.	Shall I have love for anyone else'.
117	Quant Melïons a antendu	When Melion this heard	When Melion realised
118	Que si veu erent atendu,	That if wishes were attended,	That his vows were fulfilled,
119	Par mi les flans l'a enbracie,	By him his arms her embraced,	He put his arms around her waist
120	Et plus de trente fois baisie.	And more-than of thirty times kissed.	And kissed her more than thirty times.
121	Puis a tote sa gent mandee,	Then had all his people sent-for,	Then he sent for all his people
122	L'aventure lor a contee.	The-adventure theirs he recounted.	And told them what had happened.
123	Cil ont veüe la pucele;	That they saw the maiden;	They looked at the maiden;
124	El roialme n'avoit tant bele.	The the-kingdom had-not as-much beauty.	There was none so beautiful in the kingdom.
125	A son castel l'en a mené,	To his castle her he took,	Melion took her to his castle;
126	Molt ont grant joie demené.	Much they great rejoicing of-took.	They took of great rejoicing.
127	A grant richoise l'espousa,	With great splendour her-he-married,	He married her with great splendor
128	Et molt grant joie en demena;	And much great joy in took;	And took great joy about it;
129	.XV. jors a li pas duré.	fifteen days had this passed endured.	The celebrations lasted fifteen days.
130	.III. ans le tint en grant chierté;	three years he held in great affection;	For three years he held her in great affection:
131	.II. fiex en ot en ces .III. ans,	two sons he had in the three years,	He had two sons by her in these three years

Anonymous - Melion

	Old French	Literal	English
132	Molt par en fu lies et joians.	Much by he became glad and joyful.	And was very glad and joyful about it.
133	Un jor en la forest ala;	One day in the forest he-went;	One day he went into the forest;
134	Sa chiere feme ot lui mena.	His dear wife had he taken.	He took his dear wife with him.
135	Un cerf trova, si l'ont chacié,	A stag found, and this-they chased,	He found a stag, and they chased it
136	Et il s'en fuit, le col baissié.	And it then fled, his neck lowered.	And it fled, its neck lowered.
137	.I. escuier o lui avoit	A squire with him he-had	He had a squire with him
138	Ki son bercerië portoit.	Who his quiver carried.	Who was carrying his quiver.
139	En une lande sont entré.	And a heath they entered.	They went on to a heath.
140	En .I. buisson a regardé;	And one bush he looked-upon;	Melion looked into a bush:
141	Un molt grant cerf i voit estant.	One very great stag he saw standing.	He saw a great stag standing there.
142	Sa feme regarde en riant.	His wife he-looked and laughed.	Laughing, Melion looked at his wife.
143	'Dame', fait il, 'se jo voloie,	'Lady', said he, 'if you wish,	'Lady', he said, 'if you wish,
144	.I. molt grant cerf vos mosterroie:	A very large stag you I-will-show:	I would show you a great stag:
145	Veés le la en cel buisson.'	See it there in that bush'.	See it there in that bush'.
146	'Par foi!' fait ele, 'Melïon,	'By faith said she, 'Melion,	'By my faith', she said, 'Melion,
147	Sachiés se jo de cel cerf n'ai	Know-you if I of that stag do-not-have	Know that if I do not have some of that stag
148	Que jo jamais ne mangerai.'	Then I never shall-not i-will-eat'.	I shall never eat again'.
149	Del palefroi chaï pasmee,	From palfrey fell fainting,	She fell from her palfrey, fainting,
150	Et Melïons l'a relevee.	And Melion her picked-up.	And Melion picked her up.
151	Qant ne le pot reconforter,	When not he could comfort,	When he could not comfort her,
152	Molt durement prist a plorer.	Very sorely took to weeping.	She began to weep bitterly.
153	'Dame', dist il, 'por Deu merci,	'Lady', said he, 'for God's mercy,	'Lady', he said, 'for the grace of God,

Anonymous - Melion

	Old French	Literal	English
154	*Ne plorés mais, jo vos en pri.*	Not i-implore-you more, I you with pray.	Never cry, I beg of you.
155	*J'ai en ma main .I. tel anel;*	I on my hand one such ring;	I have on my hand such a ring;
156	*Ves le ci en mon doit manel.*	Se it here on my finger my-hand.	See it here on my ring-finger.
157	*.II. pieres a ens el caston:*	two stones has on its casting:	It has two stones in its casting:
158	*Onques si faites ne vit on;*	Never such work no-one saw of;	No-one has ever seen such work;
159	*L'une est blance, l'autre vermeille.*	Of-one is white, the-other crimson.	One stone is white, the other crimson.
160	*Oïr en poés grant merveille:*	Hear of may great marvel:	You may hear a great marvel of them:
161	*De la blance me toucerés*	Of the white me touch	You will touch me with the white stone
162	*Et sor mon chief le meterés*	And on my head it place	And place it on my head
163	*Qant jo serai despoilliés nus,*	When I will-be unclothed nude,	When I am undressed and nude,
164	*Leus devenrai, grans et corsus.*	Wolf I-shall-become, great and strong.	And I shall become a great strong wolf.
165	*Por vostre amor le cerf prendrai*	For your love the stag capture	For love of you, I shall capture the stag
166	*Et del lart vos aporterai.*	And of the-article you I-shall-bring.	And bring some of its meat back to you.
167	*Por Deu vos pri, ci m'atendés*	For God to-you I-pray, here wait-for-me	I pray you, for God's sake, wait for me here
168	*Et ma despoille me gardés.*	And my clothes mine guard.	And guard my clothing.
169	*Je vos lais ma vie et ma mort:*	I you leave my life and my death:	I leave you my life and my death:
170	*Il n'i auroit nul reconfort*	There never have none recovery	There will be no recovery
171	*Se de l'autre touciés n'estoie;*	If of the-other touched I-shall-not-be;	If I am not touched with the other stone;
172	*Jamais nul jor hom ne seroie.'*	Never not day a-man nor become'.	I should never again be a man'.
173	*Il apela son escuier,*	He called his squire,	He called his squire,
174	*Si le commande a deschaucier.*	Him he commanded to remove-boots.	And commanded him to remove his boots.
175	*Cil vint avant, sel descaucha,*	He came forward, him removed-boots,	He came forward, removed the boots

Anonymous - Melion

	Old French	Literal	English
176	Et Melïon el bois entra.	And Melion in the-forest entered.	And Melion went into the woods.
177	Ses dras osta, nus est remez,	His clothes removed, nude, he remained,	He removed his clothes, remained nude,
178	De son mantel s'est afublez.	Of his cloak he-is wrapped.	And wrapped himself in his cloak.
179	Cele l'a de l'anel touchié	This she of the-ring touched	She touched him with the ring
180	Qant le vit nu et despoillié.	When she saw nude and unclothed.	When she saw him nude and undressed.
181	Lors devint leu grant et corsus:	Then became wolf great and strong:	Then he became a great and strong wolf:
182	En grant paine s'est enbatus.	In great suffering he-is entangled.	He had got himself into deep trouble.
183	Li leus s'en vait, molt tost corant	The wolf then went, very quickly running	The wolf set out, running quickly
184	La ou il vit le cerf gisant;	There where he saw the stag lying;	To where he saw the stag lying;
185	Tost se fu en la trace mis.	Immediately he became on the trace set.	He set himself to the scent at once.
186	Anchois sera grant li estris	In-choice there-will-be great his strife	There will be great strife before
187	Que il l'ait pris ne adesé,	For he has seized or approached,	He has captured or approached it
188	Ne que il avra del lardé.	Nor which he has of the-meat.	Before he has any of the meat.
189	La dame dist a l'escuier:	The lady said to the-squire:	The lady said to the squire:
190	'Or le laissons assés chacier'.	'Now him let-us very-well hunt.	'Now let him hunt for a while'.
191	Montee est, plus ne se targa,	Mounted she, more not she delayed,	She mounted, delayed no longer,
192	Et l'escuier o lui mena.	And the-squire with her took.	And took the squire with her.
193	Droit vers Yrlande, sa contree,	Directly towards Ireland, her-own country,	Straight towards Ireland, her own country,
194	En est la dame retornee.	And was the lady returned.	The lady returned.
195	Al havene vint, nef i trova;	In harbour went, ship she found;	She went to the harbour, found a ship
196	As mariniers tantost parla	The mariners immediately spoke-to	And soon spoke to the crew
197	Qui l'ont mené a Duveline,	Who they took to Dublin,	Who took her to Dublin,

Anonymous - Melion

	Old French	Literal	English
198	Une cité sor la marine,	A city on the sea,	A maritime city,
199	Qui son pere ert, le roi d'Yrlande;	Which her father was, the king of-Ireland;	Which belonged to her father, the King of Ireland;
200	Des or ot ce qu'ele demande.	Of-them now had that which-she asked-for.	Now she had what she required.
201	Lués qu'ele fu al port venue,	As-soon-as which-she came to the-port arrived,	As soon as she came into the port
202	A grant joie fu receüe.	With great joy was received.	She was welcomed with great joy.
203	De li lairomes aïtant,	Of her we-leave at-this-point,	We will leave her at this point,
204	De Melïon dirons avant.	Of Melion wel-tell further.	And tell further about Melion.
205	Melïon, ki le cerf chaça,	Melion, who the stag chased,	Melion, who was chasing the stag,
206	A grant merveille le hasta.	He great intensely it harried.	Harried it intently.
207	En la lande l'a conseü,	To the heath this pursued,	He pursued it on to a heath,
208	Tot maintenant l'a abatu,	All at-once this brought-down,	And at once he brought it down;
209	Puis prist de lui .I. grant lardé;	Then seized of him a great piece-of-meat;	Then he took a large piece of meat from it;
210	En sa bouche l'en a porté.	In his mouth he it carried.	He carried it away in his mouth.
211	Hastivement s'en retorna	Quickly he returned	He quickly went back
212	La ou il sa feme laissa,	There where he his wife left,	To where he had left his wife,
213	Mais il ne l'i a pas trovee;	But he not her then not found;	But he did not find her there;
214	Vers Yrlande s'en est tornee.	To Ireland was she returned.	She had set out for Ireland.
215	Molt fu dolans, ne set que face,	Very-much became sad, not knowing what to-do,	He was very sad and did not know what to do
216	Qant il ne le troeve en la place.	When he not her found in that place.	When he could not find her in that place.
217	Mais neporqant, se leus estoit,	But even-though, he wolf was,	But even though he was a wolf,
218	Sens et memoire d'ome avoit.	Sense and memory of-a-man he-had.	He retained the reason and memory of a man.
219	Tant atendi k'il avespra.	Until waited he-for evening-fell.	He waited until evening fell.

Anonymous - Melion

	Old French	Literal	English
220	Une nef vit que on charga,	A ship saw which being loaded,	He saw a ship being loaded
221	Ki la nuit devoit eskiper	Which that night was-to sail	Which was to sail that night
222	Et en Yrlande droit aler.	And to Ireland directly go.	And go directly to Ireland.
223	Envers cele part s'en ala,	Towards this part he-did go,	He made his way there
224	Tant atendi k'il anuita.	Until waiting for-the night-fall.	And waited until night fell.
225	Entrés i est par aventure,	Entered he this by adventure,	He took a risk and boarded it,
226	Car de sa vie n'avoit cure.	For of his live he-did-not-have care.	For he cared nothing for his life.
227	Sos une cloie s'est muciés	Under an enclosure he-is hidden	He concealed himself beneath an enclosure,
228	Et s'est tapis et enbuissiés.	And is hidden and embedded.	Crouched down and was hidden.
229	Li maronier se sont hasté,	The mariners of made haste,	The mariners made haste
230	Car molt avoient bon oré.	Because very they-had fair wind.	For they had a fair wind.
231	Lors s'en tornerent vers Yrlande;	Then they turned towards Ireland;	Then they turned towards Ireland;
232	Cascuns avoit quanque demande.	Each had what-he asked-for.	Each of them had what he wished.
233	Il sachierent amont lor voiles;	They hoisted up their sails;	They hoisted up the sails
234	Al ciel corent et as estoiles,	Of the-skies steered and the stars,	And steered by the sky and the stars,
235	Et l'endemain a l'ajornee	And the-morning of the-next-day	And the next day at dawn
236	Virent d'Yrlande la contree.	They-saw Ireland there encountered.	They saw the country of Ireland.
237	Et qant il sont al port venu,	And when it they to the-port came,	And when they had come into harbour,
238	Melïon n'a plus atendu,	Melion could-not more wait,	Melion waited no longer;
239	Ains issi fors de son cloier,	Rather thus out of his enclosure,	He came out from his bench
240	De la nef sailli el gravier.	Of there the-ship leapt he to-the-ground.	And leapt from the boat on to the shingle.
241	Li maronier l'ont escrié	The mariners to-him-they shouted	The sailors shouted at him

Anonymous - Melion

	Old French	Literal	English
242	*Et de lor aviron geté.*	And of their oars threw.	And threw their oars at him.
243	*Li uns l'a d'un baston feru,*	Of-them one his of-a stick struck,	One of them struck him with a stick
244	*A poi k'il ne l'ont retenu;*	And little could-he not they catch;	And they nearly managed to catch him;
245	*Lies est qant lor fu escapés.*	Happy he-was when from-them became escaped.	He was glad when he had escaped from them.
246	*Sor une montaigne est alés;*	Upon a mountain he went;	He went up a mountain
247	*Molt a regardé le païs*	Much he looked-at the country	And looked closely at the country
248	*Ou il savoit ses anemis.*	Where he knew his enemies.	Where he knew his enemies to be.
249	*Encore avoit il son lardé*	Still had he his piece-of-meat	He still had his piece of meat,
250	*Ke de sa terre ot aporté;*	Which of his country had carried;	Which he had brought from his own land;
251	*Grant faim avoit, si l'a mangié,*	Great hunger had, so he ate,	He was very hungry, so he ate it,
252	*Molt l'avoit la mer traveillié.*	Much had the sea exhausted.	The sea crossing had exhausted him.
253	*En une forest est alés,*	He a forest was went-to,	He went into a forest,
254	*Vaches et bues i a trovés.*	Cows and oxen there he found.	And found cows and oxen there.
255	*Molt en ocit et estrangla;*	Many of-them killed and strangled;	He killed and strangled many of them;
256	*Iluec sa guerre comencha.*	There his war began.	There he began his war.
257	*Plus en i a ocis de cent*	More of he had killed than a-hundred	He killed more than a hundred of them
258	*A cest premier commencement.*	At this early stage.	At this early stage.
259	*La gent ki estoit el boscage*	There people who were in the-woods	The people who lived in the woodland
260	*Virent des bestes le damage;*	Saw of-them beasts he harmed;	Saw their beasts harmed;
261	*Corant vindrent a la cité,*	Running they-went to the city,	They went running to the city,
262	*Al roi l'ont dit et aconté*	To-the king they said and recounted	Spoke to the king and said
263	*Qu'en la forest .I. leu avoit*	which there forest a wolf was	That there was a wolf in the forest,

Anonymous - Melion

	Old French	Literal	English
264	Ki le païs tot escilloit.	Which the land all ravaged.	Which was ravaging all the land.
265	Molt a ocis de lor almaille;	Many of killed of their animals;	It had killed many of their livestock;
266	Mais tot ce tient li rois a faille.	But all this thought the king of failed.	But all this thought the king nothing of.
267	Tant a alé par la forest,	So-much had gone by the forest,	Melion went so far through the forest,
268	Par montaignes et par dessert,	By mountains and by wasteland,	Through the mountains and the wasteland,
269	Que a .X. leus s'acompaigna:	That was Ten wolves accompanied:	That he was joined by ten wolves;
270	Tant les blandi et losenga	So-much he cajoled and persuaded	He cajoled and persuaded them so much
271	Que avoec lui les a menés,	That with him he had taken,	That he took them with him
272	Et font totes ses volentés.	And they-did all he wished.	And they did all he wished.
273	Par le païs molt se forvoient,	By the countryside much they went,	They went roaming through the countryside
274	Homes et femes malmenoient.	Men and women attacked.	And attacked men and women.
275	Un an tot plain ont si esté:	One year all full they thus were:	For a full year they were like this:
276	Tot le païs ont degasté,	All the country they laid-waste,	They laid waste all the country,
277	Homes et femes ocioient;	Men and women killed;	Killed men and women
278	Tote la terre destruioient.	All the land destroyed.	And destroyed all the land.
279	Molt se savoient bien gaitier;	Very-much they knew well protect;	They knew how to protect themselves well;
280	Li rois nes pooit engingnier.	The king not could trick.	The king could not trick them.
281	Une nuit orent molt erré,	One night had-they much roamed,	One night they had roamed widely
282	Traveillié furent et pené.	Exhausted they-were and weary.	And were exhausted and wearied.
283	En .I. bois joste Duveline,	In one forest next-to Dublin,	There was a wood near Dublin,
284	Sor .I. tertre les la marine -	On a mound by the sea	On a mound next to the sea
285	Li bois estoit les une plaigne	The wood was by a plain	The wood was near a plain,

Anonymous - Melion

	Old French	Literal	English
286	Tot environ ot grant compaigne -	Completely surrounded with large fields	Completely surrounded by open countryside
287	Por reposer i sont entré.	For rest there they entered.	And they entered it to rest themselves.
288	Traï seront et engané:	Betrayed the-will-be and tricked:	They will be betrayed and tricked:
289	Un païsant les a veüs;	One peasant them of saw;	A peasant saw them,
290	Al roi en est tantost corus.	To the-king then was immediately ran.	And at once ran to the king.
291	'Sire', dist il, 'el bois reont	'Sire', said he, 'in the-forest round	'Sire', he said, 'in the round wood
292	Li .XI. leu colchié s'i sont.'	They eleven wolves laid-up they are'.	The eleven wolves have laid up'.
293	Qant li rois l'ot, molt en fu liés;	When the king heard, much he became happy;	When the king heard it, he was very glad,
294	Ses homes en a araisniés.	His men he had called.	And he addressed his men.
295	Li rois ses homes apela.	The king his men addressed.	The king called his men.
296	'Baron', dist il, 'entendés cha!	'Barons', said he, 'listen to-me	'Barons', he said, 'listen to me.
297	Sachiés de voir les .XI. lous	Know-you the truth this eleven wolves	Know in truth that this man here
298	En ma forest vit cis hom tous.'	In my forest saw this man all'.	Has seen all eleven wolves in my forest'.
299	Les rois dont soelent les pors prandre	The nets they-had only the boars to-catch	They had the nets, which they used to capture boar
300	Environ le bois ont fait tendre.	Around the forest they were out-stretched.	Stretched around the woods.
301	Qant on les ot tot portendus,	When they the with all stretched-out,	When they had been all stretched out,
302	Lors monta, n'i atarga plus.	He mounted, not delaying more.	He mounted and did not delay any longer.
303	Sa fille dist avoec venra	His daughter said with would-go	His daughter said she would go with him
304	Et la chace des leus verra.	And the hunting of-the wolves watch.	And watch the hunting of the wolves.
305	Tantost se sont el bois alé,	Immediately of they the woods went,	At once they went to the wood,
306	Tot coiement et a celé;	All secretly and of hidden;	In complete secrecy and well hidden;
307	Le bois ont tot aviroré,	The forest they all surrounded,	They surrounded the wood completely,

Anonymous - Melion

	Old French	Literal	English
308	Car gent i ot a grant plenté	Because people there with was a-great many	For there were a great many people
309	Ki portent haces et maçues,	Who carried axes and cudgels,	Who carried axes and cudgels,
310	Et li alqant espees nues.	And they some swords bared.	And some had swords bared.
311	Adont i ot .M. chiens hués	Now there with A-thousand hounds excited	Now there were a thousand excited hounds,
312	Ki les leus orent tost trovés.	Which the wolves heard immediately found.	Which quickly found the wolves.
313	Melïon vit k'il ert traïs:	Melion saw that-he was betrayed:	Melion saw that he was betrayed:
314	Bien set que il est malbaillis.	Well knew that he was in-trouble.	He understood that he was in trouble.
315	Li chien les vont molt angoissant	The dogs they went very aggressively	The dogs went for them viciously
316	Et il vienent as rois fuiant.	And they came in the-nets running.	And they came fleeing into the nets.
317	Tot sont detrancié et ocis;	All were cut-up and killed;	All were cut to pieces and killed;
318	Un tos seus n'en escapa vis	One all single not escape knew	Not a single one of them escaped alive,
319	Fors Melïon, qui escapa,	Except Melion, who escaped,	Save for Melion, who fled
320	Par deseure les rois lança.	By only the nets leaping.	By leaping over the nets.
321	En .I. grant bois s'en est alé;	Then a great wood he was gone;	He went into a great wood;
322	Par engien lor est escapé.	By ingenuity his had escaped.	He had escaped by his ingenuity.
323	A la cité sont repairié;	To the city they went;	The hunters went back to the city;
324	Li rois se fait durement lié.	The king he became very pleased.	The king was very pleased.
325	Li rois grant joie demena	The king great joy took	The king felt great joy
326	Que il des .XI. leus .X. a,	That he of eleven wolves Ten had,	That he had ten of the eleven wolves,
327	Car molt bien s'est vengié des leus;	For very well he avenged of-the wolves;	So he had avenged himself well on the wolves:
328	Escapés ne l'en est c'uns seus.	Escaped only of-them was one alone.	Only one of them alone had escaped.
329	Sa fille dist: 'C'est li plus grans;	His daughter said: 'this he most large;	His daughter said: 'This one was the largest;

Anonymous - Melion

	Old French	Literal	English
330	Encor les fera tos dolans'.	Still he will-make all regret.	He will still make them all regret it'.
331	Qant Melïon fu escapés,	When Melion had escaped,	When Melion had escaped,
332	Sor une montaigne est montés;	Over a mountain he mounted;	He climbed a mountain;
333	Molt fu dolans, molt li pesa	Much became unhappy, much he-was troubled	He was very unhappy and troubled
334	De ses leus que il perdu a.	Of his wolves which he lost had.	About his wolves, which he had lost.
335	Molt a traveillié longement,	Much had-he suffered a-long-time,	For a long time he had suffered,
336	Mais ore avra socors briement:	But soon will-he-have help shortly:	But in a short while now he will have help:
337	Artus en Yrlande venoit,	Arthur to Ireland came,	Arthur was coming to Ireland,
338	Car une pais faire i voloit.	Because a peace-treaty to-make he wished.	For he wished to make a peace treaty.
339	Mellé estoient el païs,	Conflicts there-were in the-land,	There were conflicts in the land
340	Acorder vout les anemis.	Agreement wished he to-bring.	And he wished to bring agreement to the factions;
341	Sor les Romains voloit conquerre;	Over the Romans he-wanted-to conquer;	He wanted to conquer the Romans,
342	Mener les voloit en sa guerre.	To-take them he-wished to this war.	He wanted to lead them in his war.
343	Li rois venoit priveement,	The king went privately,	The king was travelling privately,
344	Ne menoit mie molt grant gent:	Not many at-all many great people:	He did not bring very many people;
345	.XX. chevaliers od lui menoit.	twenty knights with him brought.	He brought with him twenty knights.
346	Molt fist bel tans, bon vent avoit,	Very-much was well the-weather, good wind had,	The weather was fine, they had a good wind;
347	Molt fu la nef et riche et grans.	Many became there ship and splendid and large.	The ship was both splendid and large
348	Il i avoit bons esturmans;	He with had good steersman;	And there was a good steersman;
349	Molt par fu bien apareillie,	Very-well by was well equipped,	It was very well equipped
350	D'ommes et d'armes bien garnie.	of-men and arms well supplied.	And supplied with men and arms.
351	Lor escus furent fors pendus.	Their shields were outside hanging.	Their shields were hung over the side.

Anonymous - Melion

	Old French	Literal	English
352	Melïons les a coneüs.	Melion them of recognised.	Melion recognised them.
353	Primes conut l'escu Gawain	First recognised the-shield Gawain's	First he recognised Gawain's shield,
354	Et puis a ravisé l'Iwain	And then he noticed Yvain's	And then he noticed Yvain's,
355	Et puis l'escu le roi Ydel;	And then the-shield the king Ydel;	And then King Ydel's shield;
356	Tot ce li plot et li fu bel.	All this him delighted and he became pleased.	All this delighted him and was pleasing to him.
357	L'escu le roi bien ravisa;	the-shield the king's well recognised;	He recognised the king's shield easily;
358	Sachiés de voir grant joie en a.	Knew of truly greay joy he had.	Know truly that he was very joyful because of this:
359	Molt en fu liés, molt s'esjoï,	Very was he happy, much rejoicing,	He was very happy about it and rejoiced greatly,
360	Car encor quide avoir merci.	Because still believed have mercy.	For he believed he would have mercy.
361	Vers la terre vienent siglant,	Towards the land they-came sailing,	They came sailing towards the land,
362	Li vens lor est venus devant,	But the-wind them was veering before,	But the wind veered in front of them.
363	Ne porent prendre cil le port;	Not could take they the harbour;	They could not reach the harbour;
364	Adont i ot grant desconfort.	Thus he had great discomfort.	Now Melion had great despair.
365	A .I. autre port sont torné,	Then An other port they turned-to,	They turned towards another port,
366	A .II. lieues de la cité.	That two leagues from the city.	Two leagues from the city.
367	Un grant castel i ot jadis,	One great castle there was in-days-passed,	Once there was a great castle there,
368	Mais ore estoit tos agastis,	But now was all ruined,	But now it was all ruined,
369	Et qant il furent arivé	And when they had arrived	And when they arrived
370	Nuis estoit, si ert avespré.	Night was, and was dark.	It was night, it was dark.
371	Li rois s'est al port arivés.	The king he-was to-the port arrived.	The king reached the port.
372	Molt s'est traveilliés et penés	Very-much he-was tired and suffering	He was very tired and suffering
373	Car la nef li ot fait grant mal.	Because the ship him had made very ill.	Because the ship him had made very ill.

Anonymous - Melion

	Old French	Literal	English
374	Il apela son senescal.	He called his steward.	He called his steward.
375	'Alés', dist il, 'la fors veïr	'Go', said he, 'there outside see	'Go', he said, 'and see out there
376	U jo porrai anuit gesir.'	Where I could tonight lie'.	Where I can sleep tonight'.
377	Cil est a la nef retornés;	He was to there the-ship returned;	Then he went back to the ship
378	Les canberlens a apelés.	The chamberlains he called.	And called the chamberlains.
379	'Issiés', fait il, 'ça fors od moi,	'Come', do it, 'thus outside with me,	'Come on land with me', he said,
380	Si atornés l'ostel le roi.'	Thus prepare lodging the king'.	And prepare lodging for the king'.
381	Fors de la nef en sont issu,	Outside of the ship of they went,	Outside of the ship of they went,
382	Si en sont a l'ostel venu.	This with went to lodging went.	And came to the lodging.
383	.II. chierges i ont fait porter,	two torches there they had carried,	They had two torches carried there
384	Molt tost les firent alumer.	Very quickly them had illuminated.	And quickly had them illuminated.
385	Kieutes i portent et tapis,	Quilts they carried and carpets,	They carried quilts and carpets
386	Hastivement fu bien garnis.	Quickly preparing well furnishing.	And quickly prepared furnishings well.
387	Adont s'en est li rois issus;	Thus then was the king left;	Then the king left the ship
388	Droit a l'ostel en est venus,	Straight to lodging then was came,	And came straight to the lodging,
389	Et qant il i fu ens entré	And when he there became in entered	And when he had gone in
390	Liés est qant si bel l'a trové.	Happy was when thus well this found.	He was glad to find it all so pleasant.
391	Melïons pas ne se targa:	Melion not no-longer he delayed:	Melion did not hesitate:
392	Tostans contre la nef ala.	Went towards the ship along.	He went at once towards the ship.
393	Pres de la chasvie est arestus;	Close of the castle he stopped;	He halted near the castle
394	Molt les a bien reconeüs.	Very-much they he well recognised.	And recognised them very well.
395	Bien set se del roi n'a confort	Well knew he of-the-king not-having comfort	He well knew, if he had no comfort from the king,

Anonymous - Melion

	Old French	Literal	English
396	Qu'en Yrlande prendra la mort.	that-in Ireland would there die.	That he would die in Ireland;
397	Mais il ne set comment aler,	But he not knew how-to proceed,	But he did not know how to proceed:
398	Leus est et si ne set parler.	Wolf was and thus not knew speech.	He was a wolf and could not speak.
399	Et nekedent tostans ira,	And nevertheless went-forwards at-once,	Nevertheless he would go forward at once,
400	En aventure se metra.	And risked his life.	And risk his life.
401	A l'uis le roi en est venus;	Then he-came-to the king and was come;	He came to the king's door;
402	Tot ses barons a coneüs.	All the barons he recognised.	He knew all the barons.
403	Il ne s'est de rien arestés;	He not was of nothing stopping;	He did not stop for a moment,
404	Tot droit al roi en est alés,	All directly to-the king was he went,	But went directly up to the king,
405	En aventure est de morir.	And risked he of death.	Although it might mean his death.
406	As piés le roi se lait chaïr,	At the-feet the king he had fallen,	He let himself fall at the king's feet
407	Ne se voloit pas redrecier;	Not he wished not to-get-up;	And would not rise again;
408	Dont la veïsciés merveillier.	Then there would-have-seen amazement.	Then you would have seen amazement there.
409	Ce dist li rois: 'Merveilles voi!	This said the king: 'Marvels I-see	The king spoke thus: 'I can see marvels!
410	Cis leus est ci venus a moi.	The wolf has here come to me.	This wolf has come here to me.
411	Or sachiés bien qu'il est privés.	Now know well which is tame.	Now know well that he is tame.
412	Mar ert touchiés ne adesés.'	Wrongly to touch or approach'.	Wrong to anyone who touches or approaches him'.
413	Qant li mangier sont apresté	When the meal was ready	When the meal was ready,
414	Et li barons orent lavé,	And the barons soon washed,	And the barons soon washed,
415	Li rois lava, si s'est assis;	The king washed, thus was seated;	And the king washed and sat down;
416	Devant ax ont les dobliers mis.	In-front to-the they the plates set.	The dishes were placed before them.
417	Li rois a Ydel apelé,	The king to Ydel called,	The king called to Ydel

Anonymous - Melion

	Old French	Literal	English
418	Se l'assist joste son costé.	He seated next-to his side.	And sat him at his side.
419	As piés le roi jut Melïons;	At feet the king's lay Melion;	Melion lay at the king's feet
420	Bien conut trestot les barons.	Well recognised all the barons.	And recognised all the barons well.
421	Li rois le regarda sovent.	The king him glanced-at often.	The king glanced at him often.
422	Un pain li done et il le prent,	One piece-of-bread he gave and he it received,	He gave Melion a piece of bread and he took it;
423	Puis le commença a mangier.	Then he began to eat.	Then he began to eat it.
424	Li rois s'en prist a merveillier;	The king was seized with marvel;	The king began to marvel at this;
425	Al roi Ydel dist: 'Esgardés!	To-the king Ydel said: 'Look!	He said to King Ydel: 'Look!
426	Sachiés que cis leus est privés'.	Know-you that this wolf is tame.	You can be sure this wolf is tame'.
427	Li rois .I. lardé li dona	The king one piece-of-meat him gave	The king gave Melion a piece of meat
428	Et il volentiers le manga.	And it gladly he ate.	And he ate it gladly.
429	Lors dist Gavains: 'Segnor, veés;	Then said Gawain: 'My-lords, look;	Then Gawain said: 'My lords, look;
430	Cis leus est tous desnaturés'.	This wolf is completely unnatural.	This wolf is completely unnatural'.
431	Entr'aus dïent tot li baron	amongst said all the barons	All the barons said amongst themselves
432	C'ainc si cortois leu ne vit on.	as-this so courteous a-wolf not seen one.	That no-one had never seen such a well-mannered wolf.
433	Li rois fait aporter le vin	The king had brought him wine	The king had wine brought
434	Devant le leu en .I. bacin.	Before the wolf in a basin.	Before the wolf in a basin.
435	Li leus le voit, beüt en a;	The wolf this saw, drank of it;	The wolf saw it and drank some;
436	Sachiés que molt le desira	Know-you that much he desired	You may be sure he wanted it very much,
437	Qu'il a del vin assés beü,	which he from wine well drank,	For he drank deeply of the wine,
438	Et li rois l'a molt bien veü.	And the king this very well watched.	And the king watched him closely.
439	Qant del mangier furent levé	When from the-meal had risen	When they had risen from the meal

Anonymous - Melion

	Old French	Literal	English
440	Et li baron orent lavé,	And the barons now washed,	And the barons had washed,
441	Fors issirent sor le gravoi.	Outside they-went to the shore.	They went out on to the shore.
442	Tostans fu li leus ot le roi;	Always was the wolf with the king;	The wolf was always with the king;
443	Onques ne sot cel lieu aler	Never not knew the place to-go	He did not know anywhere he could go
444	C'on le peüst de lui oster.	where he could of him separate.	Where he could be separated from him.
445	Qant li rois volt aler colchier,	When the king wanted to-go retire,	When the king wanted to retire,
446	Son lit rova apareillier.	His bed ordered prepared.	He ordered his bed to be prepared;
447	Dormir s'en vait, molt est lassés,	To-sleep then went, very much tired,	He went to sleep, he was very tired,
448	Et li leus est od lui alés,	And the wolf was with him went,	And the wolf went with him;
449	Ainc nel pot on de li partir,	Rather none could they of him leave,	No-one could make him leave him;
450	As piés le roi en vait gesir.	At the-feet the king's then went to-lie.	He went to lie at the king's feet.
451	Li rois d'Yrlande a mes eüs	The king of-Ireland had message of-them	The King of Ireland received a message
452	C'Artus estoit a lui venus;	That-Arthur was to him come;	That Arthur had come to him;
453	Molt en fu liés, grant joie en a.	Very-much he became glad, greatly rejoiced then he.	He was very glad and rejoiced greatly.
454	Bien main a l'aube se leva,	Well morning at dawn he rose,	He rose very early at dawn
455	Deci al port en est alés;	Went to-the harbour then he went;	And went to the harbour,
456	Ses barons a o lui menés,	His barons he with him took,	Taking his barons with him;
457	Tot droit al port en vint errant.	All directly to the-harbour then came were.	They all made directly for the harbour.
458	Molt s'entrefirent bel samblant;	Much greeting well mannered;	They greeted each other in a friendly manner;
459	Artus li mostra grant amor	Arthur him showed great love	Arthur showed him great love
460	Et fait li a molt grant honor.	And did him a very great honour.	And did him great honour.
461	Qant il le voit a lui venir,	When he him saw the king coming,	When he saw the King of Ireland coming towards him,

Anonymous - Melion

	Old French	Literal	English
462	*Ne se volt mie enorgoillir,*	Not he wished not-at-all haughty,	He did not wish to appear haughty,
463	*Ains leva sus, si l'a baisié.*	Rather stood up, thus him embraced.	But stood up and embraced him.
464	*Li ceval sont apareillié;*	The horses were prepared;	The horses were ready;
465	*Ne targent plus, ains sont monté,*	Not delayed more, rather they mounted,	They delayed no longer, but mounted,
466	*Ore en iront vers la cité.*	Now them rode towards the city.	Then rode them towards the city.
467	*Li rois monte en son palefroi,*	The king mounted then his palfrey,	The king mounted his palfrey
468	*Se son leu a pris bon conroi.*	He his wolf then took good care-of.	And took good care of his wolf;
469	*Ne le voloit mie laissier;*	Not he wished not-at-all to-leave;	He did not wish to leave him behind.
470	*Il fu tos jors a son estrier.*	He became all day at his stirrup.	All the time Melion was at his stirrup.
471	*D'Artus fu molt li rois joians,*	Arthur became very-much the king joyed,	The king was very happy to see Arthur,
472	*Li conrois fu riches et grans.*	The company was splendid and large.	The company was large and magnificent.
473	*A Duveline sont venu*	To Dublin they came	They came to Dublin
474	*Et el grant palais descendu.*	And in great palace dismounted..	And dismounted at the great palace.
475	*Qant li rois monta el doignon,*	When the king went-up in the-keep,	When the king went up into the keep,
476	*Li leus li tint par le giron;*	The wolf him went by his robe;	The wolf held him by the skirt of his robe;
477	*Qant li rois Artus fu assis,*	When the king Arthur was seated,	When King Arthur was seated,
478	*Li leus s'est a ses piés mis.*	The wolf was by his feet set.	The wolf placed himself at his feet.
479	*Li rois a son leu regardé;*	The king to his wolf looked;	The king looked at his wolf;
480	*Joste le dois l'a apelé.*	Close he must be called.	He called him near to the table.
481	*Ensamble sisent li doi roi,*	Together sat the two kings,	The two kings sat together;
482	*Molt par i ot riche conroi,*	Very-much by there with splendid company,	The company was splendid,
483	*Molt bien servoient li baron;*	Very well served the barons;	The barons waited on them very well:

Anonymous - Melion

	Old French	Literal	English
484	De totes pars par la maison	Of all parts by the dwelling	In all parts of the dwelling
485	Servi furent a grant plenté.	Served were a great plenty.	They were served lavishly.
486	Mais Melïon a regardé;	But Melion around looked;	But Melion looked around;
487	Enmi la sale ravisa	In-the-middle there hall noticed	He noticed in the middle of the hall
488	Celui ki sa feme enmena.	He who had wife-his taken-away.	The man his wife had taken away with her.
489	Bien sot la mer estoit passés	Well knew the sea was crossed	He knew that he had crossed the sea
490	Et en Yrlande estoit alés.	And in Ireland was gone.	And had gone to Ireland.
491	Par l'espaule le vait saisir:	By his-shoulder he went to-seize:	He went to seize him by the shoulder:
492	Cil ne se pot a lui tenir;	He not him could off him hold;	The man could not keep him at bay;
493	En la sale l'a abatu.	In the hall he attacked.	Melion attacked him in the hall:
494	Ja l'eüst mort et confondu,	Already would-have killed him destroyed,	He would have soon killed and destroyed him
495	Ne fuissent li sergant le roi	Not was-it-not-for the servants the king's	Had it not been for the king's servants,
496	Qui la vindrent a grant desroi;	Who there saw the great commotion;	Who saw the great commotion;
497	De totes pars par le palais	From all parts by the palace	From all parts of the palace
498	Fus aporterent et gamais.	Were brought and sticks.	They carried sticks and cudgels.
499	Ja eüsent le leu tué,	Already would-have the wolf killed,	They would certainly have killed the wolf
500	Qant li rois Artus a crié,	When the king Arthur he cried,	When King Arthur cried out:
501	'Mar ert touchiés', fait il, 'par foi!	'Wrong who touches, does him, 'by faith!	'Wrong to anyone who touches him', he said, 'by my faith!
502	Sachiés que li leus est a moi'.	Know-you that the wolf is of mine.	Know that this wolf is mine'.
503	Dist Ydel, li fiex Yrïen:	Said Ydel, the son-of Yrien:	Ydel, son of Yrien, said:
504	'Segnor, ne faites mie bien;	'My-lords, not doing not-at-all well;	'My lords, you are not doing right at all;
505	S'il nel haïst, nel touchast pas',	if-he did-not hate-him, nor touched-him not,	If the wolf had not hated him, he would not have touched him',

Anonymous - Melion

	Old French	Literal	English
506	Et dist li rois: 'Ydel, droit as'.	And said the king: 'Ydel, right is.	And the king said: 'Ydel, you are right'.
507	Artus s'en est del dois tornés;	Arthur then was from the-table turned-away;	Arthur moved away from the table,
508	Deci al leu en est alés,	And-then to-the wolf then he went,	And went right up to the wolf.
509	Al vallet dist: 'Tu jehiras	To-the servant said: 'You-will confess	He said to the servant: 'You will confess
510	Porcoi t'a pris ou ja morras'.	Why you-he seized or at-once die.	Why he seized you or you shall die at once'.
511	Melïons le roi regarda;	Melion the king looked-at;	Melion looked at the king;
512	Celui estraint et il cria.	He gripped and he cried-out.	He gripped the servant and he cried out.
513	Cil a le roi merci rové;	He then the king's mercy begged;	He begged the king for mercy,
514	Dist k'il contera verité.	Saying that-he would-recount the-truth.	Saying that he would tell him the truth.
515	Maintenant a le roi conté	At-once he the king recounted	At once he told the king
516	Comment la dame l'ot mené,	How the lady before he-took,	How the lady had brought him with her,
517	Comment del anel le toucha	How of-the ring she touched	How she had touched Melion with the ring,
518	Et en Yrlande l'en mena.	And then Ireland him-there took.	And taken him there to Ireland.
519	Tot li a dit et coneü	All he had said and made-known	All this he said and made known,
520	Comment li estoit avenu.	Just as it-was happened.	Just as it had happened.
521	Artus a le roi apelé:	Arthur then the king called:	Arthur addressed the King of Ireland,
522	'Or sai bien que c'est verité;	'Now I-know well that it-is true;	'Now I know well that this is true;
523	De mon baron m'est il molt bel.	Of my baron mine-is he very-much beloved.	I am very happy about my baron.
524	Faites moi delivrer l'anel	Have to-me brought the-ring	Have the ring brought to me
525	Et vo fille, ki l'enporta;	And your daughter, which it-took-away;	And your daughter, who took it away;
526	Malvaisement engignié l'a.'	Evil tricked she-has'.	She has played an evil trick on him'.
527	Li rois s'en est d'iluec tornés,	The king then was from-there turned-away,	The King of Ireland left there;

Anonymous - Melion

	Old French	Literal	English
528	En sa cambre s'en est entrés;	To his chamber then he entered;	He went into his chamber,
529	Le roi Ydel o lui mena.	The kinf Ydel with him took.	Taking King Ydel with him.
530	Tant le blandi et losenga	So-much he cajoled and persuaded	He cajoled and persuaded his daughter so much
531	Qu'ele li a l'anel doné;	that-she to-him then the-ring gave;	That she gave him the ring;
532	Il l'a al roi Artu porté.	He this to-the king Arthur brought.	He brought it to King Arthur.
533	Si tost con l'anel a veü,	As soon-as recognised the-ring he saw,	As soon as he saw the ring,
534	Melïon l'a bien coneü;	Melion this well recognised;	Melion recognised it well;
535	Al roi vint, si s'agenoilla	To-the king went, so kneeling	He went to the king, fell on his knees
536	Et andeus les pies li baisa.	And both his feet he kissed.	And kissed both his feet.
537	Li rois Artus le vout touchier;	The king Arthur him wanted to-touch;	King Arthur wanted to touch him,
538	Gavains nel volt pas otroier.	Gawain not willed not agree-to.	But Gawain would not permit it.
539	'Biaus oncles', fait il, 'non ferés!	'Good uncle, said he, 'don't do	'Good uncle', he said, 'don't!
540	En une chambre l'en menrés,	Into a chamber him take,	Take him to a chamber
541	Tot seul a seul priveement,	All alone by himself privately,	In absolute privacy
542	Que il n'ait honte de la gent'.	That he is-not shamed of the people.	So that he is not shamed in front of people'.
543	Li rois a Gavain apelé,	The king of Gawain called,	The king called Gawain,
544	Si a od lui Ydel mené,	And he with him Ydel took,	And he took Ydel with him;
545	En une cambre l'en mena.	To a chamber he-him took.	He led Melion to a chamber.
546	Qant il fu ens, l'uis si ferma,	When he was inside, was thus closed,	When he was inside, he closed the door.
547	L'anel li a sor le chief mis;	the-ring he to above his head set;	He put the ring to Melion's head;
548	D'ome li aparut le vis,	of-a-man to-him appeared his face,	His face appeared like a man's,
549	Tote sa figure mua.	All his person mutated.	All his body changed.

Anonymous - Melion

	Old French	Literal	English
550	Lors devint hom et si parla.	Then became man and then spoke.	Then he became a man and spoke.
551	As pies le roi se lait cheïr;	At-the feet-of the king he then fell;	He let himself fall at the king's feet;
552	D'un mantel le firent covrir.	of-a mantle he-was made covered.	They wrapped him in a cloak.
553	Qant le virent home formé,	When this they-saw the-man formed,	When they saw him shaped as a man,
554	Molt ont grant joie demené.	Many they great joy took.	They felt very great joy.
555	De pitié li rois en plora,	Of pity the king then wept,	The king wept for pity over him
556	Et en plorant li demanda	And in weeping him asked	And weeping asked him
557	Comment li estoit avenu,	How it was happened,	How this had happened to him;
558	Par pechié l'avoient perdu.	By misfortune had lost.	Through misfortune they had lost him.
559	Son canberlenc a fait mander,	His chamberlain he had called-for,	He had his chamberlain sent for,
560	Riches dras li fist aporter;	Rich clothes he had brought;	And had rich clothing brought to him;
561	Bien le vesti et conrea	Well he dressed and cultivated	He dressed Melion and turned him out well
562	Et en la sale le mena.	And in the hall they took.	And took him into the hall.
563	Merveillié sont par la maison	Marvel they by the dwelling	Throughout the dwelling they marvelled
564	Qant voient venir Melïon.	When they-saw coming Melion.	When they saw Melion coming.
565	Li rois a sa fille amenee.	The king then his daughter brought.	The king brought his daughter.
566	Al roi Artus l'a presentee,	To-the king Arthur he presented,	He presented her to King Arthur,
567	A tote sa volenté faire,	As all how he-wished to-do,	To do with as he wished,
568	Voille l'ardoir, voille desfaire.	Wishing torn-to-pieces, wishing to-do.	Whether to burn her or have her torn to pieces.
569	Melïons dist: 'Jel toucherai	Melion said: 'I shall-touch	Melion said: 'I shall touch her
570	De la piere, ja nel lairai'.	Of the stone, me nothing shall-stop.	With the stone, nothing will stop me'.
571	Artus li a dit: 'Non ferés!	Arthur to-him then said: 'Don't do!	Arthur said to him: 'Don't!

	Old French	Literal	English
572	*Por vos beaus enfans le lairés.'*	For your beautiful children her let-be'.	For the sake of your beautiful children, let her be'.
573	*Tot li baron l'en ont proié;*	All the barons him they begged;	All the barons begged it of him;
574	*Melïon lor a otroié.*	Melion their of granted.	Melion granted their wish.
575	*Li rois Artus tant demora*	The king Arthur until delayed	Arthur remained there
576	*Que la guerre tot acorda.*	When the war was-all in-accord.	Until the war was settled.
577	*En sa contree en est alés,*	Then his country he was going,	Then he set out for his own land,
578	*Melïon a od lui menés;*	Melion then with him took;	Taking Melion with him;
579	*Molt en fu liés, grant joie en a.*	Very-much he became glad, great joy at it.	Melion was very glad, he rejoiced at it.
580	*Sa feme en Yrlande laissa:*	His wife in Ireland he-left:	He left his wife in Ireland.
581	*A deables l'a commandee;*	To the-devil he-her commended;	He commended her to the devil;
582	*Jamais n'iert jor de li amee,*	Never another day of he loved,	She would never again be loved by him
583	*Por ce qu'ele l'ot si bailli,*	Because that which-she before so burdened,	Because she had mistreated him so badly,
584	*Con vos avés el conte oï.*	As you have in the-recounting heard.	As you have heard in the tale.
585	*Ne le volt il onques reprendre,*	No-longer her willed he never take-back,	He never wished to take her back,
586	*Ains le laissast ardoir u pendre.*	Rather her let-be burned or hanged.	He would like to have let her burn or be dismembered.
587	*Melïon dist: 'Ja ne faldra*	Melion said: 'Indeed never fail	Melion said: 'It will never fail to happen
588	*Que de tot sa feme kerra,*	Which of completely his wife believes,	That he who believes his wife completely
589	*Qu'en la fin ne soit malbaillis;*	will there end he let-be badly-done;	Will be ruined in the end;
590	*Ne doit pas croire tos ses dis'.*	He should not believe all she says.	He should not believe all she says'.
591	*Vrais est li lais de Melïon,*	True is the lay of Melion,	The Lay of Melion is true,
592	*Ce dïent bien tot li baron.*	So they-say well all the barons.	As all the nobles say.
593	*Explicit de Melïon*	Now-is-the-end of Melion	This is the end of Melion.

Anonymous - Melion

Old French	Literal	English
594 Chi fine Melïon	Here ends Melion	Here ends Melion.

Word List *(Old French to English)*

Old French	English
A, a	
a	a, against, and, around, as, at, by, had, had-he, has, he, in, is, it, of, off, on, that, the, then, this, to, under, up to, was, with
abatre	destroy, knock down
abatu	attacked, brought-down
abevrez	drink
aconté	recounted
acorda	in-accord
acorder	agreement
acreanter	agree, allow, promise
ad	against, in, on, to, up to
adenz	face downwards
adesé	approached
adesés	approach
adober	arm oneself
adont	now, thus
adurer	worship
afaire	matter
afublez	wrapped
agastis	ruined
ai	have, have-I
aidier	to-help
aiglantier	wild rose
aiglent	wild rose
ainc	earlier, rather
ains	earlier, rather
ainz	earlier, rather
aire	appearance
aise	facility
aistre	be
aïtant	at-this-point
al	at, in, of, the, to, to-the
ala	along, go, he-went, of, of-the, went
alaine	blast, breath
alé	going, gone, went
aleine	blast, breath
aler	go, proceed, to-go
alés	go, going, gone, went, went-to
alez	go, gone, went
alkun	some
almaille	animals
alme	somebody, soul
alne	ell
alout	he-went, went
alqant	some
alques	somewhat
alt	high, important, strong
altain	deep, high
altre	other
altresi	also
alum	let-us
alumer	illuminated
ama	he-loved
amant	lover
ame	somebody, soul
amé	loved
amee	loved
amenee	brought
amer	love, loved, to-love
amerai	shall-I-love
amez	a-love, loved
ami	friend
amie	friend
amis	friend
amistié	friendship
amont	up
amor	love
amot	loved
an	year
anchois	in-choice
andeus	both
anel	ring
anemis	enemies, to-bring

Word List (Old French to English)

Old French	English
angoissant	aggressively
angregier	become more painful, grow worse
anima	soul
anme	somebody, soul
anor	esteem, fief, honor, respect
anpur	for the sake of
ans	years
antendu	heard
anuit	tonight
anuita	night-fall
aparant	visible
aparceüz	aware
apareillie	equipped
apareillié	prepared
apareillier	prepared
aparut	appeared
apela	addressed, called, he-called
apelé	called
apeler	accuse, call, summon
apelés	called
apercevoir	know, notice
apert	manifest, open, visible
aporté	carried
aporter	brought
aporterai	I-shall-bring
aporterent	brought
apres	after, afterwards
aprés	after
apresté	ready
araisniés	called
ardoir	burn, burned
ardre	burn
arestés	stopping
arestus	stopped
argent	money, riches, silver
ariere	back, to-him
arire	back
arivé	arrived
arivés	arrived
ariver	arrive
arme	somebody, soul
arrere	back
arriere	back
art	craft, liberal art
Artu	Arthur (a name)
Artus	Arthur (a name)
as	at, at-the, have, in, is, the, you
asailli	assailed
aseüré	assured
asez	many, much, very well
asopli	downcast
asproier	prosecute, torment
assanler	assemble, call together, meet
assembler	assemble, call together, meet
asseoir	lay siege, place, set up
assés	many, much, very well, very-well, well
assez	rather
assis	seated
astenir	keep from
ataindre	catch, reach, regain
atarga	delaying
atendi	waited, waiting
atendu	attended, wait
atorna	returned
atorner	prepare, turn
atornés	prepare
atot	with
aturnez	dressed
aucun	some
auroit	have
aussi	also, likewise
aut	high, important, strong
autre	other
avant	forward, further
avec	with
aveir	be, have
aveit	had, he-had
avenant	attractive, beautiful
avenantment	attractively
avenement	arrival
avenir	arrive, frequently, happen

Word List (Old French to English)

Old French	English
aventure	adventure, risked
avenu	happened
avenue	happened
avés	have
avespra	evening-fell
avespré	dark
aviler	abandon, disgrace
avint	happened
aviron	oars
avironé	surrounded
aviser	appreciate, look at, recognize, see
avoc	with
avoec	with
avoient	they-had
avoir	be, have
avoit	had, he-had, was
avra	has, will-he-have
avreie	could
avrez	have
avuec	with
avum	have-we
ax	to-the

B, b

Old French	English
bacheler	knight, page, young knight aspirant, young man
bachelor	page, young knight aspirant, young man
bacin	basin
bailli	burdened
baillier	give, own, receive
bailliz	treated
baisa	kissed
baise	kisses
baisie	kissed
baisié	embraced
baisier	kiss
baissié	lowered
balt	full of fervor, happy
barbe	beard
baron	baron, barons, brave knight, brave warrior
barons	barons
barun	barons
baruns	barons
baston	stick
bataille	battle
beals	handsome
bealz	gentle
beaus	beautiful
beax	beautiful
bec	beak
bel	beautiful, beloved, dear, handsome, pleased, well
bele	beautiful, beauty, elegant, fair-lady
belement	politely
ben	good, good fortune, well-being
ber	baron
bercerië	quiver
beste	beast, the-beast
bestes	beasts
beü	drank
beüt	drank
bevre	drink
biaus	good
bien	good, good fortune, many, much, really, well, well-being
Bisclavret	Bisclavret (a name), werewolf
blanc	white
blance	white
blandi	cajoled
blonde	blonde
bois	forest, forests, the-forest, tree, wood, woods
bon	fair, good
bone	good
bonement	very-well
bons	good
bonté	excellence
bos	forest, tree
boscage	the-woods
boscages	woods
bouche	mouth

Word List (Old French to English)

Old French	English
braire	shout, sing
Bretaigne	Brittany (a place)
Bretan	Breton (a place)
briement	shortly
buche	mouth
bues	oxen
buisson	bush
buissun	bush

C, c

Old French	English
c	a-hundred
cadable	catapult
c'ainc	as-this
cambre	chamber
canberlenc	chamberlain
canberlens	chamberlains
canbres	chambers
car	because, for
c'artus	that-Arthur
cas	affair, event, fall
cascuns	each
castel	castle
caston	casting
cavee	dug-out
ce	he, it, so, that, this
ceanz	in here
cel	that, the, this
cela	concealed
cele	such, that, that-time, the, this
celé	hidden
celer	conceal
celes	hide, those
cels	those
celui	for-him, he, that-one, who-him
cent	a-hundred, a-hundred
ceo	behold-this, everyone, it, such, that, this
cerf	stag
cervel	brains
ces	the
cest	this
c'est	it-is
ceste	this
ceu	it, that, this
ceval	horses
cez	these
cha!	to-me
chaça	chased
chace	hunting
chacerai	will-hunt
chacié	chased
chaciee	chased
chacier	hunt, the-hunt
chaciez	chase
chaeir	fall
chaï	fell
chaïr	fallen
chaitif	miserable
chaloir	concern, matter
chambre	chamber, chamber, room, royal apartment, territory
chambres	rooms
chant	melody, song
chanter	sing
chapele	chapel
char	flesh, meat
charga	loaded
charn	flesh, meat
chartre	agreement, letter
chasez	fief
chasser	hunt
chastel	castle
chasvie	castle
cheïr	fell
chemin	path
cheoir	fall
cher	beloved, expensive
chevalerie	chivalry, knights
chevalier	knight, the-knight
chevaliers	gentleman, knight, knights
chevauchie	expedition, ride
cheveleüre	hair
chi	here
chief	head, the-end
chien	dogs
chiens	dogs, hounds

Word List (Old French to English)

Old French	English
chier	love, loved
chiere	dear, dearly-love
chierges	torches
chierté	affection, fondness
choisi	saw
chose	affair, creature, thing
chrestien	christian
ci	here
ciel	heaven, the-skies
cil	he, him, that, the-one, they, this, this-he
cis	the, this
cist	the-last, this
cit	city, town
cité	city
citet	city, town
clameor	appeal
clamer	call, confess, proclaim
clementiam	grace
clerc	clerk
clerge	clerk
clers	clear
cloie	enclosure
cloier	enclosure
coer	heart
coiement	secretly
cointe	clever, elegant, refined
col	neck, shoulders
colchié	laid-up
colchier	retire
colomb	dove, pigeon
colon	dove, pigeon
colpe	mistake, sin
com	as, in order that, when
comandé	commanded
comander	give, order, recommend
comencha	began
comencier	begin, start
coment	how, somehow
commande	commanded
commandee	commended
comme	as, when
commença	began
commencement	stage
comment	how, how-to, just
compaigne	fields, troops
compaignie	company
comunalment	together
con	as, recognised
c'on	where
concreidre	give in
coneü	made-known, recognised
coneüs	recognised
confondu	destroyed
confort	comfort
congié	leave, permission, permission to leave
conqueroit	conquered
conquerre	capture, conquer
conrea	cultivated
conroi	care-of, retinue, the-trappings
conrois	retinue
conseilleor	advisor, counsellor
conseillier	advisor, counsellor
conserrer	deprive, resign
conseü	pursued
consirrer	deprive, resign
consolation	consolation
conte	count, the-recounting
conté	recounted
conteça	contented
contee	recounted
contenant	appearance, demeanour, expression
conter	count, relate
contera	would-recount
conterent	heard
contre	against, compared with, to-greet, towards
contredire	oppose, resist
contree	country, encountered
conut	recognised
converse	about
conversez	about
convoier	escort
cope	mistake, sin

Word List (Old French to English)

Old French	English
cor	heart, horn
corant	running
corent	steered
corn	horn
corocier	afflict, anger
corpe	mistake, sin
corre	run
cors	body, heart
corsus	strong
cortois	courteous, courtly
cortoise	courtly
cortoisie	courtesy
corus	ran
cose	affair, creature, thing, things
costé	side
cosu	sewn
couchier	lie down
covrir	covered
creanter	agree, grant
creeit	believed
creistre	grow
creü	believed
cria	cried-out
crie	asks-for
crié	cried
criem	fear
crier	shout
croire	believe
croistre	grow
cruese	hollow
cuer	heart, my-heart
cuidier	think
cuire	burn, cook
culchier	slept
cum	as, as-though, how, in order that, with
cument	what
cumfaitement	in-such-way
cumpaignuns	companions
cuneüz	known
cunfort	comfort
cungié	leave
cunquerre	capture, conquer
c'uns	one
cunseil	counsel
cunseilla	counselled
cunta	recounted
cunté	recounted
cunteneit	led-himself
cunter	to-recount
cuntredit	opposition
cuntree	country
curage	heart
cure	a-care, anxiety, care
curios	careful
curt	court
curteis	courteous
cururent	chased
curut	anger, he-runs, ran, running
curuz	anger

D, d

Old French	English
daignier	deign
dales	along, next to
dalles	along, next to
dam	lord, sir
damage	harm, harmed, trouble
dame	dame, lady, madam, woman
damoiselle	girl of noble birth
dan	lord, sir
d'armes	arms, of-arms
d'Artus	Arthur (a name)
de	by, from, of, out-of, than, the, to, with
de vers	from the direction of, in the direction of
deable	devil
deables	the-devil
debonaire	noble, sweet
deci	and-then, went
deciré	tear
deçoivre	deceive, mislead
dedenz	inside
deduire	lead, live
deduit	pleasure
degasté	laid-waste
degré	staircase

Word List (Old French to English)

Old French	English
dei	finger, owe
del	from, of, of-the, of-this, to
delé	next to; beside
deleiz	next to; beside
deles	next to; beside
delicios	delicious
delivrer	brought
d'els	be
demain	the-morning
demanda	asked, questions
demandasse	to-ask
demandast	asked-for
demande	asked, asked-for
demandé	asked
demander	ask, ask for
demandez	ask, sought-for
demeine	own
demena	took
demené	of-took, took
demora	delayed
demoree	delay, stay
demorer	remain, stay
demostrer	explaine, indicate, show
denz	teeth
departi	departed
depescié	dismembered
dermine	of-ermine
des	of, of-the, of-them
descaucha	removed-boots
descendre	descend, dismount
descendu	dismounted.
deschaucier	remove-boots
desconfire	defeat, demolish
desconfort	discomfort
descoplé	unleashed
descovri	revealed
descuplé	released
deseure	only
desevrer	to-separate
desfaire	to-do
desi	until
desira	desired
desnaturés	unnatural
desos	under
desous	under
despoille	clothes
despoillié	unclothed
despoilliés	unclothed
despueille	clothes, the-clothing
desroi	commotion
dessert	wasteland
destreit	difficulty
destresce	distress
destruioient	destroyed
detrancié	cut-up
deu	god, god's
deüst	had, would
devant	before, in front of, in the presence of, in-front
deveneit	became
devenir	become
devenrai	I-shall-become
devenus	become
devenuz	became-of
devers	from the direction of, in the direction of
devez	should
deviene	become
devient	becomes
devindrent	became
devint	became
devoir	have to
devoit	was-to
devorer	devour
devure	devours
di	day, say, tell
diavle	devil
die	you
dïent	said
dïent	said, they-said, they-say
d'iluec	from-there
dirai	tell, will-tell
dire	say, tell
direit	tells
dirons	wel-tell
dis	says, tell
dist	said, saying, tell
dit	said

Word List (Old French to English)

Old French	English
dites	tell
divers	various
dobliers	plates
doi	finger, two
doignon	the-keep
dois	must, the-table
doit	finger, should
dol	grief, suffering
dolans	regret, sad, sorrow, unhappy
dolent	sorrowful, wetched
dolor	pain, suffering
dolur	pain
dolz	gentle, sweet
d'ome	of-a-man
d'ommes	of-men
dona	gave
donc	then, therefore
done	gave
doné	gave
doner	give, given
donrai	i-will-give
dons	gifts
dont	of which, of whom, of-where, of-whom, then, they-had, whose
dormant	sleeping
dormir	to-sleep
doter	be afraid, doubt
dous	gentle, sweet, two
dras	clothes
dreit	straight
droit	direct, directly, proper, right, straight
drue	mistress
duc	duke
duel	grief, suffering
dulz	sweet
d'ume	of-a-man
d'un	of-a
duna	gave
dunc	so
d'une	of-one, with-a
duné	dedicated
dunt	of which, of whom, which, whose
dur	cruel, hard, unrefined
duré	endured
durement	greatly, hard, sorely, very
durrai	grant
duter	doubt
dutez	doubt
duveline	Dublin (a place)
dyrlande	of-Ireland
d'yrlande	from-Ireland, Ireland (a place), of-Ireland

E, e

Old French	English
e	and, by, of, that
ed	and
eim	love
eissil	ruin, wretchedness
el	he, in, its, she, the
ele	he, she
element	energy, force, god
emparenté	of noble lineage
empedement	persecution
empeindre	blow, protrude
empereor	emperor
en	and, at, go, he, in, into, is, of, of it, of-it, of-them, on, on top of, on-which, them, then, to, unto, was, with
enamé	he-loved
enbatus	entangled
enbracie	embraced
enbracier	to-embrace
enbuissiés	embedded
encoloree	coloured
encombrer	overload
encontre	against, to, towards
encontrer	meet
encor	still, yet
encore	still, yet
encuntré	encountered
end	subsequently
endreit	immediately, precisely, right, ways
enemi	devil, enemy

Word List (Old French to English)

Old French	English	*Old French*	English
enfans	children	*entendu*	heard
enfanz	children	*entent*	listen
enferm	crippled, ill, unhealthy, weak	*entente*	reason
		entier	entire
enfermeté	illness, physical or moral weakness	*entiers*	entire
		entra	entered
enfern	hell	*entr'aus*	amongst
engagier	commit	*entre*	among, between, in the midst of
engané	tricked		
engeignier	deceive, invent, seduce	*entré*	entered
		entrepris	unhappy person
engeindre	cause	*entrerent*	entered
engendrer	cause	*entrés*	entered
engien	cheating, ingenuity, skill	*enui*	pain, torment
		envers	towards
engignié	tricked	*environ*	around, surrounded
engignier	deceive, invent, seduce	*erbre*	grass
		erent	were
engin	cheating, skill	*errant*	were
engingnier	trick	*erré*	roamed
enhaïrent	they-hated	*errer*	to-go
enmena	taken-away	*ert*	to, was, who
enmi	in-the-middle	*es*	in-those
enne	not	*esbai*	frightened, surprised, troubled
ennui	grief		
enoi	pain, torment	*esbanir*	amuse
enor	esteem, fief, honor, respect	*esbanoier*	enjoy
		escapa	escape, escaped
enorgoillir	haughty	*escapé*	escaped
enorter	exhort, seduce, urge	*escapés*	escaped
enpur	for the sake of	*escavie*	charming
enquis	inquired, queried	*eschec*	booty, loot
enragié	furious	*eschecs*	chess
enragiez	enraged	*esciënt*	it-seems
ens	in, inside, on	*escïent*	knowledge
ensamble	together	*escilloit*	ravaged
enseigna	indicated	*escolter*	listen to, pay attention to
enseigne	war cry		
enseignier	inform, point out, teach	*escouta*	listen
		escremir	fence
ensemble	together, with	*escrié*	shouted
ensemble od	together with	*escrier*	cry out, shout
ensi	so-as-this	*escrimer*	fence
ent	subsequently	*escu*	shield
entendés	listen	*escuier*	squire
entendre	hear, pay attention, try, understand	*escuiers*	squire

Word List (Old French to English)

Old French	English
escus	shields
esfrei	fear
esgardés	look
esguardez	look-at
eskiper	sail
eslais	assault
esleecier	rejoice
esmaier	be dismayed
esnasees	noselessly
espauleüre	shoulders
espee	sword
espees	swords
espés	thick
espleitiez	hurry
esposer	marry
espuse	wife
espusee	married
esracha	snatched
essil	ruin, wretchedness
est	are, are, he, is, that, was, had, has, he, he-was, is, it-is, much, she, that, this, was
estait	standing
estant	standing
esté	be, been, had-been, was, were
esteit	he-was, noble, stayed, was-he
ester	be, remain, stand, was
estes	are
estoient	there-were, they-were
estoiles	stars
estoit	it-was, was, were
estor	battle, noise, tumult
estorm	battle, noise, tumult
estraint	gripped
estrangla	strangled
estre	be, condition, life, way of life
estrié	stirrup
estrier	stirrup
estris	strife
estude	study, zeal
estudie	study, zeal
esturmans	steersman

Old French	English
estut	stand
et	and, him
euc	this
eure	hour, time
eüs	of-them
eüsent	would-have
eüsse	were
eüst	would-have
eüz	they-had
ex	eyes
explicit	now-is-the-end

F, f

Old French	English
face	to-do
fai	let
faille	failed
faim	desire, hunger
faire	do, done, made, make, to-do, to-make
faiseit	made
faisoient	they-were-making
faisoit	was-made
fait	became, did, do, does, done, had, has-done, made, said, were
faites	doing, done, have, make, makes, word
faldestoed	folding chair for important person, throne
faldestuef	folding chair for important person, throne
faldestuel	folding chair for important person, throne
faldra	fail
fals	false
faus	false
favele	lie, story
fei	faith, honor
feindre	do nothing, shy away
feintise	deceit, pretense
feiz	nothing, put, time, times

Word List (Old French to English)

Old French	English
felunie	felony
feme	wife, wife-his
femes	women
femme	the-wife, wife, woman
femmes	women
fenir	end, stop
fer	iron, weapon
fera	will-make
fereit	doing
ferés	do
ferés!	do
ferez	will-do
ferma	closed
feru	struck
feruz	beaten
feste	party
fet	act, had, said
feu	family, fire
fez	composed
fiance	promise
fief	fief
fier	fierce, proud, strong
fiere	hit
fiex	son-of, sons
figure	character, form, person
fil	son
filer	spin
fille	daughter
filuel	godson, son
fin	end
fine	ends
finir	end, stop
firent	had, made
fist	be, been-so, had, has-it, was
flans	arms
flor	flower
florir	flower
foi	faith, honor
foi!'	faith
fois	times
fol	crazy
foler	harm
font	they-did
forest	forest
forestier	foresters
forez	forests
forfait	committed
formé	formed
forment	greatly, very, very much
fors	except, out, outside
fort	fierce, hard, strong
forvoient	went
fou	family, fire
fraindre	break
frans	engaging
freindre	break
frere	brother
fromage	cheese
fu	became, came, had, happened, he, is, preparing, so, was
fuiant	running
fuier	abandon, flee from
fuir	abandon, flee from
fuissent	was-it-not-for
fuit	fled
furent	had, he-had, they-were, were
fus	were
fusse	had-been
fussent	would-be
fust	had, was

G, g

Old French	English
gab	jest
gaitier	protect
gamais	sticks
gant	glove
garant	defense, protection
garder	guard, watch over
gardés	guard
gardoient	kept
garent	defense, protection
garnement	decorative object
garnie	supplied
garnis	furnishing
garulf	werewolf

Word List (Old French to English)

Old French	English	*Old French*	English
gavain	Gawain (a name)	ha	ha, hello
gavains	Gawain (a name)	haces	axes
gawain	Gawain's	haï	hated
gent	beautiful, fair, handsome, people, race	haine	hatred
		haïst	hate-him
		halberc	hauberk
gente	elegant	halt	high, important, strong
gentil	brave, noble		
gesir	lie, to-lie	hardi	bold, brave
geté	threw	hasta	harried
geter	reject, throw, utter	hasté	haste
giron	robe	hastif	swift
gisant	lying	hastivement	quickly
gisir	to-lie	haut	high
giter	reject, throw, utter	have	dark, sick, somber
gloire	glory	havene	harbour
glorious	glorious	herbergier	lodge, receive as guest, shelter
grabatum	simple bed		
grans	great, large	herberja	he-stayed
grant	a-great, great, greatly, greay, large, tall, very	het	hates
		hom	a-man, man
granter	agree, grant	home	man, the-man
granz	grand	homes	men
gravier	to-the-ground	honestét	honor
gravoi	shore	honor	honour
gré	Greek (a name)	honore	honored
gri	Greek (a name)	honors	honour
grieu	Greek (a name)	honte	disgrace, shame, shamed
griu	Greek (a name)		
guaires	much	hors	except, out, out of
gualdine	forest	huem	a-man, man
guarde	attention	hués	excited
guardent	guard	hui	this-day
guarderent	guarded	huit	eight
guardez	take-care	huitaves	octave
guarie	relieved	hum	he, him
guerpir	abandon, abandoning, leave	hume	man
		humes	men
guerre	trouble, war	hunte	shame
guerredoner	reward	hus	doors
guise	manner, way		
gunfanuner	standard bearer		

H, h

I, i

i	a, an, he, i, is, one, she, there, they, with

Word List (Old French to English)

Old French	English
ice	this
icel	one
iceste	this
ici	here
iestre	be
ii	two
iii	three
il	has, he, him, it, there, they
ilec	there
ille	island
iluec	there
iluoc	there
ira	at-once
ire	anger, distress
iré	angry, distressed, furious
irié	angry, distressed, furious
iront	rode
isle	island
issi	happened, here, so, thus
issiés	come
issil	ruin, wretchedness
issir	come out, go out
issirent	they-went
issu	went
issus	left
itel	the-same

J, j

Old French	English
ja	already, at once, at-once, ever, I, indeed, me, never, now
jadis	days-passed, in-days-passed
jai	already, at once, now
j'ai	I
jamais	never
jambe	leg
je	I
jehiras	confess
jel	I, I-will
j'entent	i-understand
jeo	I
jes	I
jesu	Jesus (a name)
jeu	I
jo	I, me, you
joer	play
joi	joy
joians	joyed, joyful
joie	joy, rejoiced, rejoicing
joieus	full of joy
joius	joyous
jol	I
jor	a-day, day
jorn	day
jornee	day's journey
jors	day, days
joste	close, next-to
jou	I
jur	that-day
jurs	days
jusqu'a	as far as, up to
jut	lay

K, k

Old French	English
kar	because, come, therefore
ke	which
kerra	believes
ki	him, of, that, which, who
kieutes	quilts
k'il	could-he, for-the, he-for, that, that-he, which-he

L, l

Old French	English
la	had, her, his, is, it, of, she-has, that, the, there, to-the
l'a	be, he, he-her, her, him, his, she, that, this
l'acola	he-embraced

Word List (Old French to English)

Old French	English	Old French	English
l'acole	embraces	*le*	he, her, he-was, him, his, it, one, she, the, they, this, who
l'ai	have, of-him		
laid	harm		
lairai	shall-stop	*leal*	legitimate, loyal
lairés	let-be	*lee*	wide
lairomes	we-leave	*legier*	light, light-hearted, supple
lais	lay, lays, leave		
laissa	he-left, left	*l'en*	he, he-him, her, here, him, him-there, of-them, there
laissast	let-be		
laissier	abandon, leave, left, let, to-leave		
		l'endemain	the-morning
laissons	let-us	*lenporta*	it-took-away
laissuns	let-us-leave	*l'enveia*	she-sent-for
lait	had, then	*les*	by, he, her, his, let, the, them, they, this
l'ait	has		
l'ajornee	the-next-day	*l'escu*	the-shield
l'altre	the-other	*lescuier*	the-squire
l'amerent	him-loved	*l'escuier*	the-squire
lameront	him-they-would-love	*l'espaule*	his-shoulder
l'amout	him-loved	*lespousa*	her-married
lança	leaping	*leu*	a-wolf, wolf, wolves
lande	heath, land	*leur*	their
l'anel	the-ring	*leus*	wolf, wolves
l'anguissa	anguish	*l'eüssent*	they-would-have
l'apela	called	*l'eüst*	would-have
l'apelent	they-call	*leva*	rose, stood
l'aperceut	noticed	*levé*	risen
lardé	piece-of-meat, the-meat	*lever*	lift up
		levriers	greyhounds
lardoir	torn-to-pieces	*lez*	near
largece	largesse	*li*	as, but, he, her, he-was, him, his, it, of-them, she, the, they, this, to-him, was
lart	the-article		
las	lace		
lassés	tired		
l'assist	seated	*l'i*	her, him
l'aube	dawn	*lié*	happy, joyful, pleased
l'autre	the-other	*lier*	bind
lava	washed	*lies*	glad, happy
lavé	washed	*liés*	glad, happy
l'aveit	had, her-had, him-had	*liet*	happy, joyful
l'aventure	the-adventure, the-event, the-story	*lieu*	place
		lieues	leagues
l'avoient	had	*lieus*	places
l'avoit	had	*liez*	happy
l'avras	shall-have	*liges*	liege
		ligier	light, light-hearted, supple

Word List (Old French to English)

Old French	English
lignage	family, lineage
lil	lily
lit	bed
liue	mile
live	mile
livre	book, inventory
l'iwain	Yvain's
loer	praised
loër	praise
l'oï	that-heard
loial	legitimate, loyal
loier	bind
loigier	light, light-hearted, supple
loin	far, far away
loing	far, far away, long
l'oïrent	heard
lonc	far, far away, long
long	far, long
longement	a-long-time, for a long time, long
l'ont	they, this-they, to-him-they
lor	from-them, his, their, them
l'orent	had
lors	he, then
losenga	persuaded
losenja	praised
l'ostel	lodging, lodging
lot	heard
l'ot	before
l'ourent	caught
lous	wolves
lués	As-soon-as
lui	he, he, him, her, him, king
luin	far, far away
l'uis	he-came-to, was
l'une	Of-one
lung	long
lungement	long, long-after
l'unt	they
lur	let, their

M, m

Old French	English
m	a-thousand
ma	my
maçues	cudgels
magne	great
main	hand, morning
maindre	remain, stay
mains	fewer, less
maint	many, many a
maintenant	at-once, immediately, soon
mais	but, further, more, rather
maisnie	army, household
maisniee	army, household
maison	dwelling, house
maisun	home, homes, house
mal	bad, badly, disaster, evil, harm, ill, illness, mean, wretched
malbaillis	badly-done, in-trouble
malement	badly
malfé	demon, devil
malmenoient	attacked
mals	bad
maltalent	anger
malvaisement	evil
m'amur	my-love
manaça	threatened
manace	menace
manacié	threatened
manda	sent-for
mandee	sent-for
mander	called-for, commanded
mandez	ordered
maneit	lived
manel	my-hand
manga	ate
mangerai	i-will-eat
mangié	ate
mangier	eat, meal, the-meal
maniere	intention, way
manjuer	eat
manoir	a-manor
mantel	cloak, mantle

Word List (Old French to English)

Old French	English
mar	in vain, wrong, wrongly
marine	sea
mariniers	mariners
maronier	mariners
masse	mass
mat	exhausted, feeble, sad
m'atendés	wait-for-me
me	I, me, mine, to-me
mectre	put
mei	from-me, me, mine, to-me
meillor	better
meine	takes
meins	fewer, less
meinte	many
meïsmes	himself, myself
Melïon	Melion (a name)
Melïons	Melion (a name)
mellé	conflicts
mels	better, rather
memoire	memory
m'en	to-me
mena	taken, took
menace	menace
mené	he-took, took
menee	brought
mener	be-taken, lead, show, take, to-take
menés	taken, took
menestier	profession, service
menez	took
menoit	brought, many
menrés	take
mentir	betray, deny, fail, lie
mentirai	shall-lie
m'entremet	i-begin
menu	quickly
menut	quickly
mer	pure, sea
merci	grace, mercy, pity
mercie	thanks
mercïé	thanked
mere	mother
merveille	intensely, marvel, marvellously, what is surprising, wonder, wonders
merveilles	marvels
merveillié	marvel
merveillier	amazement, marvel
mes	but, furthermore, he, me, message, more, my, with
mescroire	refuse to believe, suspect
meserrez	misguided
mesfacent	harm
mesfaire	misdeed
mesfait	mistreatment
mesprendre	commit a crime, make a mistake
message	message, messenger
m'est	is, mine-is
met	go, put, puts
meterés	place
metez	place
metra	life
metre	put
mettre	put
meute	might
mi	him
mie	at-all, none-at-all, not, not-at-all
miels	better, rather
mien	among
mier	pure
millier	thousand
miracle	miracle
mis	set, treated
mise	questioned, set
moi	me, mine, to-me
moine	monk
moins	fewer, less
mollee	shaped
molt	many, much, very, very-much, very-well
mon	my
monie	monk
mont	mountain, world
monta	mounted, went-up

64

Word List (Old French to English)

Old French	English
montaigne	mountain
montaignes	mountains
monte	mounted
monté	mounted
montee	mounted
montés	mounted
moralité	character, lesson
mordre	to-bite
morir	death, die, kill
morras	die
mort	death, die, killed
mosterroie	I-will-show
mostra	showed
mot	word, words
mout	many, much, very
mua	mutated
muciés	hidden
mult	many, most, much, very
mun	my, to-me
mund	world
munte	very-important
mur	wall
mustra	commit
mut	change

N, n

Old French	English
n'a	could-not, not-has, not-has-been, not-having
n'afubla	than-worn
n'ai	do-not-have
n'ait	is-not
namai	have-I-loved
n'ameroit	enamoured
nate	matting
n'autre	or-other
n'avoit	had-not, he-did-not-have, not-having
n'avrai	shall-I
ne	and not, can, could-not, he, naught, never, no, no-longer, none, no-one, nor, not, only, or, shall-not, you
nee	born
nees	born
nef	ship, the-ship
nekedent	nevertheless
nel	among, did-not, none, nor, not, nothing
nen	do-not, not
n'en	about, do-not, nor, not, not-of
n'encontre	nor-meet
neporqant	even-though
nes	nose, noses, not
n'est	not-is
nestoie	I-shall-not-be
neveu	grandson, nephew
nevot	grandson, nephew
ni	and not, nor
n'i	never, never-will, none, No-one, not
niënt	nothing
nïent	not at all
n'iert	another
noblement	nobly
nom	name, title
nomer	call, called, name
non	don't, name, not, title
noncier	announce, tell
nonque	never
nonsavoir	ignorance
Norman	Normans (a name)
nos	we
nostre	our
n'ot	before
n'out	not-had
nu	naked
nues	bared
nuis	night
nuit	night
nul	any, anyone, no, none, not, not any
nule	any, no, not

65

Word List (Old French to English)

Old French	English
nuls	none
nun	the-name
nus	naked, us, we
nuz	nude

O, o

Old French	English
o	or, this, with
ocioient	killed
ocire	kill
ocis	killed
ocit	killed
od	among, among, with, with
odir	hear
oeuil	eye
oëz	hear, listen
of	with
oi	today
oï	heard, i-hear
oïe	you-heard
oil	eye
oir	hear
oïr	hear
oisel	bird
olifant	ivory horn
om	one
ome	man
on	being, of, one, they
oncles	uncle
onor	esteem, fief, honor, respect
onques	ever, never, once
ont	they
or	gold, just, now
oraison	prayer, speech
ore	hour, now, presently, soon, time
oré	wind
orent	had, had-they, heard, now, prayed, soon
orer	pray
orison	prayer, speech
osasse	dare
osberc	hauberk
oser	dare
osta	removed
ostee	banned
ostel	dwelling, house
oster	separate
ot	away, had, of, was, with
otrei	grant
otrier	agree, grant
otroié	granted
otroier	agree, agree-to, grant
ou	or, this, where

P, p

Old French	English
pagien	heathen, pagan
paien	heathen, pagan
paile	precious cloth
pain	bread, piece-of-bread
paine	suffering, torment
pais	peace-treaty
païs	country, countryside, land, the-country, the-land
païsant	peasant
paistre	feed
palais	palace, the-palace
palefroi	palfrey
pance	belly, stomach
paor	fear
par	by, by reason of, through
par mi	in the middle, through
parage	family, origin, rank
parament	finery, precious object
pardon	grace, permission
pardoner	forgive, pardon
parent	father, parent
parla	spoke, spoke-to, to-speak
parlé	spoken
parlement	conversation, meeting, word
parler	speak, speech, talk, to-talk-with
parleront	they-speak

Word List (Old French to English)

Old French	English
parmi	in the middle, through
parole	speech, word
pars	parts
part	part, portion
partez	part
partir	leave, part-with, to-part
partirai	will-part
parvenir	arrive
parz	sides
pas	not, passed
pasmee	fainting
passés	crossed
pau	few, little
pechié	misfortune, mistake, sin
pecier	smash to pieces
peine	suffering, torment
pendre	hang, hanged
pendus	hanging
pené	weary
pener	suffer, torture
penés	suffering
penser	pay attention, think
peor	fear
perdeit	lost, missed
perdi	lost
perdrai	destroy
perdre	lose, loss, perish
perdu	lost
perduz	lost, to-lose
pere	father
peril	danger
perir	destroy, perish
perte	destruction, fall
pes	peace
pesa	troubled, weighed-upon
pestre	feed
petit	little, small
petite	petite
peüst	could, worse
peüz	food
pié	feet, foot
piece	part, piece, segment, the-time, time
piere	prison, stone
pieres	stones
pierre	prison, stone
pies	feet, feet-of
piés	fieet, the-feet
pïés	feet
pin	pine tree
pis?	could-have
pitié	pity
place	place
plaigne	plain
plain	full
plaindre	complain, mourn, regret
plaire	please
plein	full
plenté	many, plenty
ploier	bend, yield
plora	wept
plorant	weeping
plorer	cry, shed tears, weeping
plorés	i-implore-you
plot	delighted
pluisor	several
pluisors	many
plus	another, more, more-than, most
plusor	several
plusur	many, more
plusurs	many
poeir	be able, can
poeit	can, could
poés	may
poi	but, few, little
poier	be able, can
polle	girl
pooie	could
pooir	be able, can
pooit	could
por	because, for
porchacier	pursue, seek
porcoi	why
porent	could, could-they
porofrir	present
porrai	could

Word List (Old French to English)

Old French	English
porras	may
pors	boars
port	harbour, port, the-harbour, the-port
porté	brought, carried
portendus	stretched-out
portent	carried
porter	bring, brought, carried, carry, to-bear, wear
portoit	carried
porveor	purveyor
post	after
pot	could
pou	few, little
poür	fear, horror
pout	could
poverté	misery, poverty
povre	poor
prandre	to-catch
preie	plunder
preiee	courted
preier	beg, beseech, pray
premier	earli
premiers	first
prendra	would
prendrai	capture
prendre	seize, take, take hold of
prent	received, receives
pres	close
pres de	close to
present	present
presentee	presented
presenter	bring before the judge, offer, present
prester	lend
pri	I-pray, pray
priement	prayer
prier	beg, beseech, pray
primes	first
pris	esteem, prize, seized, took
prise	taken-aside
prisier	appreciate, esteem
prison	captivity, prison
prist	pay, seized, took
priveement	privately
privés	tame
privez	close
proece	prowess
proié	begged
proisie	praised
proisier	appreciate, esteem
prous	noble
prozdum	worthy-man
pucele	girl, maiden, servant
pucelë	maiden
puceles	maidens
pui	hill, mountain
puis	after, could, since, subsequently, then
puisse	I-may
pur	all, because, by, for, therefore
purpensa	purposed

Q, q

Old French	English
qant	when
qu'a	that
Qu'ai	what-have
quanque	all that, what-he
quant	when
quar	because, for
qu'avez	which
que	for, than, that, then, what, when, which, who
quei	what
quel	what, which
qu'el	with
qu'ele	that-she, which-she
queloigne	distaff
qu'en	that-in, which, will
quenoille	distaff
quere	ask, look for, want
querre	ask, asking-for, look for, to-seek, want
querrez	ask
qu'est	what, which-is

Word List (Old French to English)

Old French	English	*Old French*	English
qui	that, what, which, who	*rei*	king, king's, stake, the-king
qu'ici	who-here	*reine*	queen
quide	believed	*reis*	king
quidot	thought	*relef*	remains, scraps
quidouent	thought-they	*relevee*	picked-up
qu'il	that, what, which, which-of, which-that	*remanoir*	remain, resist, stay
quinze	fifteen	*remembrance*	rememberance
quis	he	*remest*	more, remained
qu'um	of-him	*remez*	remained
		remire	admired

R, r

		ren	creature, person, thing
		rendi	returned
rage	rage	*rendre*	give, return
raine	queen	*rendu*	returned
raison	reason, speech, word	*renier*	abjure, deny
raisun	reason	*renoier*	abjure, deny
ravine	theft	*reont*	round
ravisa	noticed, recognised	*repaira*	returned
ravisé	noticed	*repairié*	went
ravoir	have back	*repairiez*	returned
ré	stake	*reposer*	rest
receüe	received	*reprendre*	take-back
reclamer	beg, call upon, invoke	*requerre*	ask, beseech
reconeüs	recognised	*requise*	desired
reconfort	recovery	*resort*	defense, remedy, restriction
reconforter	comfort	*resovenir*	remember
reconoistre	recognize	*respit*	delay
recorderent	repeated	*respondre*	answer
recreant	cowardly, exhausted	*respont*	responded
redoter	be afraid, fear	*respunt*	responded
redrecier	to-get-up	*retenir*	retain-him
redut	dread	*retenu*	catch, retained
refaire	repair	*retor*	return
regal	of the king, royal	*retorn*	return
regarda	glanced-at, looked-at	*retorna*	returned
regarde	he-looked	*retornee*	returned
regardé	looked, looked-at, looked-upon	*retornés*	returned
regarder	look-at-him	*reveler*	make known, reveal, revolt
regem	king	*reveste*	re-dress
regne	country, kingdom	*revienc*	return
regnoit	ruled	*rez*	stake
rehaiteroie	comfort	*rians*	sparlking
rehaitier	comfort		

Word List (Old French to English)

Old French	English
riant	laughed
riche	expensive, generous, powerful, rich, splendid, strong
richement	richly
riches	rich, splendid
richoise	splendour
rien	any, anything, creature, nothing, person, thing
rien?	nothing
riviere	rivers
roi	kinf, king, kings, king's, the-king
roialme	the-kingdom
roiauté	realm
roine	queen
roïne	a-queen, queen
rois	king, king, nets, nets, the-king, the-nets
romains	Romans (a name)
rompre	break, burst
rose	rose
rova	ordered
rové	begged
rover	ask, call upon, order
rue	street, village

S, s

Old French	English
sa	for, had, her-own, his, how, this
sachierent	hoisted
sachiés	be-sure, knew, know, know-you
sacompaigna	accompanied
s'agenoilla	kneeling
sages	understanding, wise
sai	i-know
saige	clever, educated
sailli	leapt
saint	holy
sairement	oath
saisir	to-seize
saive	clever, educated
s'alcune	if-some
sale	hall
s'alout	next-to
salu	greet
salua	greeted
saluer	greet, salute
salvage	savage
samblans	appearance
samblant	mannered
samit	rich-silk
s'amur	for-the-love-of, love
sanc	blood
sanglent	bloody
sans	without
santé	health, well-being
s'aparceit	he-perceived
s'apareillot	she-dressed
s'aresta	he-stopped
saveit	knew, knowing
s'aventure	his-adventure
savez	know
savoient	knew
savoir	know
savoit	knew
se	he, him, his, if, of, she, they, to
se coucher	lie down
se dementer	lament
se departir	go away, leave
se faire	be
se hasteier	hasten
se haster	hasten
se pasmer	faint, swoon
se reposer	rest
seans	in here
secle	earthly life, world
secorer	go to the help of
segnor	my-lords
seiez	be
seignor	lord
seignur	husband, lord, sires
seit	been, to-be
sel	him
s'el	if-she
semblance	appearance
semblant	appearance, appeared

Word List (Old French to English)

Old French	English
semblereit	would-look-like
semeine	week
sempre	always, immediately
sempres	always, immediately
sen	direction, sense
s'en	did-he, he, he-did, if, it, then, they, was, was-he, who
senescal	steward
sens	direction, sense
sentier	path
sentir	feel, smell
s'entrefirent	greeting
senz	without
seoir	be seated, sit
sera	there-will-be
serai	will-be
sereie	I-would-be
sergant	servants
seroie	become
seroit	was
seront	the-will-be
serre	prison
servant	servant
servi	served
servir	serve, served
servise	devotion, favor, service, task
servoient	served, they-served
ses	full, he, his, she, sight, the
s'esfrea	she-was-terrified
sesjoï	rejoicing
s'esmerveillent	astonished
s'est	he, he-is, he-was, is, was
set	knew, knowing, knows, seven
seü	known
seul	alone, himself, only
seule	alone, earthly life, world
seümes	knew
seur	above, on, over, sure, to
seus	alone, single
si	and, and moreover, and thus, as, but, him, his, if, so, such, that much, that way, then, this, thus, yet
s'i	they, thus
siecle	age, earthly life, world
siglant	sailing
S'il	if-he, if-him, whether
sire	husband, my-lord, sire
sis	her
sisent	sat
siwant	followed
socors	help
soelent	only
soens	his
soit	let-be
sol	alone
soloir	be accustomed
som	sleep
some	sleep
son	her, his
soner	sound, utter
sont	are, made, they, was, went, were
sor	above, on, over, to, upon
sos	under
sostenir	support, sustain
sot	found-out, knew
soure	above, on, over, to
sout	knew
sovent	frequently, many, often, time-to-time
soz	under
sucurs	help
suens	people
sui	am, i-am
suleit	used
suliëz	previously
s'umilie	is-humbled
sun	a, her, his, in
suner	sound, utter
sunt	are, they, they-were
sur	above, behind, on, over, sure, to

Word List (Old French to English)

Old French	English
sus	above, up
suventes	repeatedly
suz	above, under, up
suzprist	under-pressed
sw	vow

T, t

Old French	English
ta	your
t'a	you-he
table	game, table
tans	the-weather, time, weather
tant	as, as-much, so, so much, so-much, such, such-time, that, until
tantost	immediately
tapis	carpets, hidden
targa	delayed, waited
targent	delayed
te	you
tel	had, has, much, such
temple	forehead, temple
tendre	out-stretched
tendrement	tenderly
tenir	consider, have, hold, keep, seize
tenoit	held
tens	held, time, weather
tenu	beheld
terme	period, period of time, term
termine	period of time
terre	country, earth, land
terres	lands
tertre	mound
tes	your
teste	head
t'i	you
tient	thought
tindrent	had
tint	held, travelled, travels, went
tirer	pull
toli	taken-away
tolir	cut off, take off
toluz	took
ton	your
tor	tower
torné	turned-to
tornee	returned
torner	return, turn
tornerent	turned
tornés	turned-away
tornoier	tourney, whirl around
tort	mistake
tos	all
tost	immediately, quickly, soon, soon-as
tostans	always, went, went-forwards
tot	all, completely, entirely, every, was-all, whole
tote	all
totes	all
toucerés	touch
toucha	touched
touchast	touched-him
toucherai	shall-touch
touchié	touched
touchier	to-touch
touchiés	touch, touches
touciés	touched
tous	all, completely
trace	trace
traï	betrayed
trair	betray
traïs	betrayed
traist	drew-close
trait	draws
traïz	betrayed
travailliez	striving
traveillié	exhausted, suffered
traveilliés	tired
trei	three
treis	three
trembler	tremble
trenchier	cut
trente	thirty
trente et quatre	thirty four
tres	much, very

Word List (Old French to English)

Old French	English
tresbien	very-well
trespasser	cross, go by, pass
tresprendre	overcome completely
tresqu'	until, up to
trestot	all
tristece	horror, sadness
troeve	found
trois	three
trop	excessively, extremely, too much
trova	found
trovast	find
trové	found
trovee	found
trover	find
trovés	found
trovez	found
truevent	they-find
trusqu'	until, up to
tu	you, you-will
tucha	harm
tué	killed
tuit	all
turnez	returned
tut	all
tute	all
tutejur	all-the-day
tutes	all
tuz	all, totally

U, u

Old French	English
u	or, where, whether
ubliër	forget
ue	today
ui	today
un	a, one
unc	never
uncore	still, yet
une	a, an, one
unkes	never
uns	one
unt	then, they

V, v

Old French	English
va	went
vaches	cows
vaillant	valiant
vain	empty, weak
vairs	bright
vait	goes, went
vallet	servant
veer	forbid, refuse
veés	look, see
vei	you-see
veie	road, way
veil	old
veintre	conquer, overcome, vanquish
veïr	see
veïsciés	would-have-seen
veisins	neighbours
veïst	saw
veit	sees
veiz	time
vendra	comes
veneor	huntsmen
veneür	hunters
venez	come
vengereit	avenge-himself
vengié	avenged
vengiez	avenged
venir	come, coming, go
venoit	came, went
venra	would-go
vens	the-wind
vent	wind
venu	came, went
venue	arrival, arrived, arriving
venus	came, come, veering
veoir	see
verai	real, true
veraie	true
verde	green
verge	stick
vergier	garden, orchard
verité	the-truth, true

Word List (Old French to English)

Old French	English
veritez	true
vermeil	vermillion
vermeille	crimson
verra	watch
verruns	we-will-see
vers	against, to, toward, towards, went
vert	green
vertu	might, power, strength
ves	se
vesti	dressed
vestu	wearing
vestuz	dressed
vet	goes, there
veu	vows, wishes
veü	known-him, saw, seen, watched
veüe	saw
veus	want
veüs	saw
vie	life, live
vieil	old
vienent	came, they-came
viez	old
vif	live
vilain	bad, ugly
vin	wine
vindrent	saw, they-went
vint	came, went
virent	saw, they-saw
virge	virgin
virginitét	christian purity, spiritual purity
vis	face, knew, so
visage	face
viseter	observe, visit
vit	saw, seen
viveient	they-live
vo	your
voa	vow
voi!	I-see
voient	they-saw
voiles	sails
voille	wishing

Old French	English
voir	indeed, true, truly, truth
voirement	really
vois	go, noise, voice, word
voit	saw
voiz	noise, voice, word
voleit	wanted
volenté	he-wished, wish
volentés	wished
volentiers	gladly, he-wanted, willing, willingly
voler	fly
voloie	wish, wished
voloir	want
voloit	he-wanted-to, he-wished, wished, wished-to
volt	wanted, wants, willed, wished
vont	went
vos	to-you, you, your
vostre	your
vout	wanted, wished
voz	your
vrais	true
vueil	i-want, i-wish, want
vueille	want
vuide	empty
vuit	empty
vus	answer, i-wish, you, you-have, your, yours

X, x

x	ten
xi	eleven
xv	fifteen
xx	twenty

Y, y

Ydel	Ydel (a name)
Yrïen	Yrien (a name)
Yrlande	Ireland (a place)

Word List *(English to Old French)*

English	Old French
A, a	
a	*a, i, sun, un, une*
abandon	*aviler, fuier, fuir, guerpir, laissier*
abandoning	*guerpir*
abjure	*renier, renoier*
about	*converse, conversez, n'en*
above	*seur, sor, soure, sur, sus, suz*
a-care	*cure*
accompanied	*sacompaigna*
accuse	*apeler*
act	*fet*
a-day	*jor*
addressed	*apela*
admired	*remire*
adventure	*aventure*
advisor	*conseilleor, conseillier*
affair	*cas, chose, cose*
affection	*chierté*
afflict	*corocier*
after	*apres, aprés, post, puis*
afterwards	*apres*
against	*a, ad, contre, encontre, vers*
age	*siecle*
aggressively	*angoissant*
a-great	*grant*
agree	*acreanter, creanter, granter, otrier, otroier*
agreement	*acorder, chartre*
agree-to	*otroier*
a-hundred	*c, cent, cent*
all	*pur, tos, tot, tote, totes, tous, trestot, tuit, tut, tute, tutes, tuz*
all that	*quanque*
allow	*acreanter*
all-the-day	*tutejur*
alone	*seul, seule, seus, sol*
along	*ala, dales, dalles*
a-long-time	*longement*
a-love	*amez*
already	*ja, jai*
also	*altresi, aussi*
always	*sempre, sempres, tostans*
am	*sui*
a-man	*hom, huem*
a-manor	*manoir*
amazement	*merveillier*
among	*entre, mien, nel, od*
among, with	*od*
amongst	*entr'aus*
amuse	*esbanir*
an	*i, une*
and	*a, e, ed, en, et, si*
and moreover	*si*
and not	*ne, ni*
and thus	*si*
and-then	*deci*
anger	*corocier, curut, curuz, ire, maltalent*
angry	*iré, irié*
anguish	*l'anguissa*
animals	*almaille*
announce	*noncier*
another	*n'iert, plus*
answer	*respondre, vus*
anxiety	*cure*
any	*nul, nule, rien*
anyone	*nul*
anything	*rien*
appeal	*clameor*
appearance	*aire, contenant, samblans, semblance, semblant*
appeared	*aparut, semblant*
appreciate	*aviser, prisier, proisier*
approach	*adesés*
approached	*adesé*
a-queen	*roïne*
are	*est, estes, sont, sunt*

English	Old French
are, he, is, that, was	*est*
arm oneself	*adober*
arms	*d'armes, flans*
army	*maisnie, maisniee*
around	*a, environ*
arrival	*avenement, venue*
arrive	*ariver, avenir, parvenir*
arrived	*arivé, venue*
arriving	*venue*
Arthur (a name)	*Artu, Artus, d'Artus*
as	*a, com, comme, con, cum, li, si, tant*
as far as	*jusqu'a*
ask	*demander, demandez, quere, querre, querrez, requerre, rover*
ask for	*demander*
asked	*demanda, demande, demandé*
asked-for	*demandast, demande*
asking-for	*querre*
asks-for	*crie*
as-much	*tant*
assailed	*asailli*
assault	*eslais*
assemble	*assanler, assembler*
As-soon-as	*lués*
assured	*aseüré*
as-this	*c'ainc*
as-though	*cum*
astonished	*s'esmerveillent*
at	*a, al, as, en*
at once	*ja, jai*
at-all	*mie*
ate	*manga, mangié*
a-thousand	*m*
at-once	*ira, ja, maintenant*
attacked	*abatu, malmenoient*
attended	*atendu*
attention	*guarde*
at-the	*as*
at-this-point	*aïtant*
attractive	*avenant*
attractively	*avenantment*
avenged	*vengié, vengiez*
avenge-himself	*vengereit*
aware	*aparceüz*
away	*ot*
a-wolf	*leu*
axes	*haces*

B, b

English	Old French
back	*ariere, arire, arrere, arriere*
bad	*mal, mals, vilain*
badly	*mal, malement*
badly-done	*malbaillis*
banned	*ostee*
bared	*nues*
baron	*baron, ber*
barons	*baron, barons, barun, baruns*
basin	*bacin*
battle	*bataille, estor, estorm*
be	*aistre, aveir, avoir, d'els, esté, ester, estre, fist, iestre, l'a, se faire, seiez*
be able	*poeir, poier, pooir*
be accustomed	*soloir*
be afraid	*doter, redoter*
be dismayed	*esmaier*
be seated	*seoir*
beak	*bec*
beard	*barbe*
beast	*beste*
beasts	*bestes*
beaten	*feruz*
beautiful	*avenant, beaus, beax, bel, bele, gent*
beauty	*bele*
became	*deveneit, devindrent, devint, fait, fu*
became-of	*devenuz*
because	*car, kar, por, pur, quar*
become	*devenir, devenus, deviene, seroie*
become more painful	*angregier*

Word List (English to Old French)

English	Old French	English	Old French
becomes	devient	bread	pain
bed	lit	break	fraindre, freindre, rompre
been	esté, seit	breath	alaine, aleine
been-so	fist	Breton (a place)	Bretan
before	devant, l'ot, n'ot	bright	vairs
beg	preier, prier, reclamer	bring	porter
began	comencha, commença	bring before the judge	presenter
begged	proié, rové	Brittany (a place)	Bretaigne
begin	comencier	brother	frere
beheld	tenu	brought	amenee, aporter, aporterent, delivrer, menee, menoit, porté, porter
behind	sur		
behold-this	ceo		
being	on		
believe	croire	brought-down	abatu
believed	creeit, creü, quide	burdened	bailli
believes	kerra	burn	ardoir, ardre, cuire
belly	pance	burned	ardoir
beloved	bel, cher	burst	rompre
bend	ploier	bush	buisson, buissun
beseech	preier, prier, requerre	but	li, mais, mes, poi, si
be-sure	sachiés	by	a, de, e, les, par, pur
be-taken	mener	by reason of	par
betray	mentir, trair		
betrayed	traï, traïs, traïz		
better	meillor, mels, miels		
between	entre		
bind	lier, loier		
bird	oisel		
Bisclavret (a name)	Bisclavret		
blast	alaine, aleine		

C, c

English	Old French
blonde	blonde
blood	sanc
bloody	sanglent
blow	empeindre
boars	pors
body	cors
bold	hardi
book	livre
booty	eschec
born	nee, nees
both	andeus
brains	cervel
brave	gentil, hardi
brave knight	baron
brave warrior	baron

English	Old French
cajoled	blandi
call	apeler, clamer, nomer
call together	assanler, assembler
call upon	reclamer, rover
called	apela, apelé, apelés, araisniés, l'apela, nomer
called-for	mander
came	fu, venoit, venu, venus, vienent, vint
can	ne, poeir, poeit, poier, pooir
captivity	prison
capture	conquerre, cunquerre, prendrai
care	cure
careful	curios
care-of	conroi
carpets	tapis

Word List (English to Old French)

English	Old French	English	Old French
carried	*aporté, porté, portent, porter, portoit*	coming	*venir*
carry	*porter*	commanded	*comandé, commande, mander*
casting	*caston*	commended	*commandee*
castle	*castel, chastel, chasvie*	commit	*engagier, mustra*
catapult	*cadable*	commit a crime	*mesprendre*
catch	*ataindre, retenu*	committed	*forfait*
caught	*l'ourent*	commotion	*desroi*
cause	*engeindre, engendrer*	companions	*cumpaignuns*
chamber	*cambre, chambre, chambre*	company	*compaignie*
		compared with	*contre*
chamberlain	*canberlenc*	complain	*plaindre*
chamberlains	*canberlens*	completely	*tot, tous*
chambers	*canbres*	composed	*fez*
change	*mut*	conceal	*celer*
chapel	*chapele*	concealed	*cela*
character	*figure, moralité*	concern	*chaloir*
charming	*escavie*	condition	*estre*
chase	*chaciez*	confess	*clamer, jehiras*
chased	*chaça, chacié, chaciee, cururent*	conflicts	*mellé*
		conquer	*conquerre, cunquerre, veintre*
cheating	*engien, engin*	conquered	*conqueroit*
cheese	*fromage*	consider	*tenir*
chess	*eschecs*	consolation	*consolation*
children	*enfans, enfanz*	contented	*conteça*
chivalry	*chevalerie*	conversation	*parlement*
christian	*chrestien*	cook	*cuire*
christian purity	*virginitét*	could	*avreie, peüst, poeit, pooie, pooit, porent, porrai, pot, pout, puis pis?*
city	*cit, cité, citet*		
clear	*clers*		
clerk	*clerc, clerge*	could-have	
clever	*cointe, saige, saive*	could-he	*k'il*
cloak	*mantel*	could-not	*n'a, ne*
close	*joste, pres, privez*	could-they	*porent*
close to	*pres de*	counsel	*cunseil*
closed	*ferma*	counselled	*cunseilla*
clothes	*despoille, despueille, dras*	counsellor	*conseilleor, conseillier*
		count	*conte, conter*
coloured	*encoloree*	country	*contree, cuntree, païs, regne, terre*
come	*issiés, kar, venez, venir, venus*		
		countryside	*païs*
come out	*issir*	court	*curt*
comes	*vendra*	courted	*preiee*
comfort	*confort, cunfort, reconforter, rehaiteroie, rehaitier*	courteous	*cortois, curteis*
		courtesy	*cortoisie*

78

Word List (English to Old French)

English	*Old French*	English	*Old French*
courtly	*cortois, cortoise*	deign	*daignier*
covered	*covrir*	delay	*demoree, respit*
cowardly	*recreant*	delayed	*demora, targa, targent*
cows	*vaches*		
craft	*art*	delaying	*atarga*
crazy	*fol*	delicious	*delicios*
creature	*chose, cose, ren, rien*	delighted	*plot*
cried	*crié*	demeanour	*contenant*
cried-out	*cria*	demolish	*desconfire*
crimson	*vermeille*	demon	*malfé*
crippled	*enferm*	deny	*mentir, renier, renoier*
cross	*trespasser*	departed	*departi*
crossed	*passés*	deprive	*conserrer, consirrer*
cruel	*dur*	descend	*descendre*
cry	*plorer*	desire	*faim*
cry out	*escrier*	desired	*desira, requise*
cudgels	*maçues*	destroy	*abatre, perdrai, perir*
cultivated	*conrea*	destroyed	*confondu, destruioient*
cut	*trenchier*	destruction	*perte*
cut off	*tolir*	devil	*deable, diavle, enemi, malfé*
cut-up	*detrancié*		
		devotion	*servise*

D, d

English	*Old French*	English	*Old French*
		devour	*devorer*
		devours	*devure*
dame	*dame*	did	*fait*
danger	*peril*	did-he	*s'en*
dare	*osasse, oser*	did-not	*nel*
dark	*avespré, have*	die	*morir, morras, mort*
daughter	*fille*	difficulty	*destreit*
dawn	*l'aube*	direct	*droit*
day	*di, jor, jorn, jors*	direction	*sen, sens*
days	*jors, jurs*	directly	*droit*
day's journey	*jornee*	disaster	*mal*
days-passed	*jadis*	discomfort	*desconfort*
dear	*bel, chiere*	disgrace	*aviler, honte*
dearly-love	*chiere*	dismembered	*depescié*
death	*morir, mort*	dismount	*descendre*
deceit	*feintise*	dismounted.	*descendu*
deceive	*deçoivre, engeignier, engignier*	distaff	*queloigne, quenoille*
		distress	*destresce, ire*
decorative object	*garnement*	distressed	*iré, irié*
dedicated	*duné*	do	*faire, fait, ferés, ferés!*
deep	*altain*	do nothing	*feindre*
defeat	*desconfire*	does	*fait*
defense	*garant, garent, resort*	dogs	*chien, chiens*
		doing	*faites, fereit*

Word List (English to Old French)

English	Old French
done	*faire, fait, faites*
do-not	*nen, n'en*
do-not-have	*n'ai*
don't	*non*
doors	*hus*
doubt	*doter, duter, dutez*
dove	*colomb, colon*
downcast	*asopli*
drank	*beü, beüt*
draws	*trait*
dread	*redut*
dressed	*aturnez, vesti, vestuz*
drew-close	*traist*
drink	*abevrez, bevre*
Dublin (a place)	*duveline*
dug-out	*cavee*
duke	*duc*
dwelling	*maison, ostel*

E, e

English	Old French
each	*cascuns*
earli	*premier*
earlier	*ainc, ains, ainz*
earth	*terre*
earthly life	*secle, seule, siecle*
eat	*mangier, manjuer*
educated	*saige, saive*
eight	*huit*
elegant	*bele, cointe, gente*
eleven	*xi*
ell	*alne*
embedded	*enbuissiés*
embraced	*baisié, enbracie*
embraces	*l'acole*
emperor	*empereor*
empty	*vain, vuide, vuit*
enamoured	*n'ameroit*
enclosure	*cloie, cloier*
encountered	*contree, encuntré*
end	*fenir, fin, finir*
ends	*fine*
endured	*duré*
enemies	*anemis*
enemy	*enemi*
energy	*element*
engaging	*frans*
enjoy	*esbanoier*
enraged	*enragiez*
entangled	*enbatus*
entered	*entra, entré, entrerent, entrés*
entire	*entier, entiers*
entirely	*tot*
equipped	*apareillie*
escape	*escapa*
escaped	*escapa, escapé, escapés*
escort	*convoier*
esteem	*anor, enor, onor, pris, prisier, proisier*
evening-fell	*avespra*
event	*cas*
even-though	*neporqant*
ever	*ja, onques*
every	*tot*
everyone	*ceo*
evil	*mal, malvaisement*
excellence	*bonté*
except	*fors, hors*
excessively	*trop*
excited	*hués*
exhausted	*mat, recreant, traveillié*
exhort	*enorter*
expedition	*chevauchie*
expensive	*cher, riche*
explaine	*demostrer*
expression	*contenant*
extremely	*trop*
eye	*oeuil, oil*
eyes	*ex*

F, f

English	Old French
face	*vis, visage*
face downwards	*adenz*
facility	*aise*
fail	*faldra, mentir*
failed	*faille*

Word List (English to Old French)

English	*Old French*	English	*Old French*
faint	*se pasmer*	followed	*siwant*
fainting	*pasmee*	fondness	*chierté*
fair	*bon, gent*	food	*peüz*
fair-lady	*bele*	foot	*pié*
faith	*fei, foi, foi!'*	for	*car, por, pur, quar, que, sa*
fall	*cas, chaeir, cheoir, perte*	for a long time	*longement*
fallen	*chaïr*	for the sake of	*anpur, enpur*
false		forbid	*veer*
false		force	*element*
family	*feu, fou, lignage, parage*	forehead	*temple*
far	*loin, loing, lonc, long, luin*	forest	*bois, bos, forest, gualdine*
far away	*loin, loing, lonc, luin*	foresters	*forestier*
father	*parent, pere*	forests	*bois, forez*
favor	*servise*	forget	*ubliër*
fear	*criem, esfrei, paor, peor, poür, redoter*	forgive	*pardoner*
		for-him	*celui*
feeble	*mat*	form	*figure*
feed	*paistre, pestre*	formed	*formé*
feel	*sentir*	formerly	*ça en arriere*
feet	*pié, pies, pïés*	for-the	*k'il*
feet-of	*pies*	for-the-love-of	*s'amur*
fell	*chaï, cheïr*	forward	*avant*
felony	*felunie*	found	*troeve, trova, trové, trovee, trovés, trovez*
fence	*escremir, escrimer*	found-out	*sot*
few	*pau, poi, pou*	frequently	*avenir, sovent*
fewer	*mains, meins, moins*	friend	*ami, amie, amis*
fieet	*piés*	friendship	*amistié*
fief	*anor, chasez, enor, fief, onor*	frightened	*esbai*
		from	*de, del*
fields	*compaigne*	from the direction of	*de vers, devers*
fierce	*fier, fort*	from-Ireland	*d'yrlande*
fifteen	*quinze, xv*	from-me	*mei*
find	*trovast, trover*	from-them	*lor*
finery	*parament*	from-there	*d'iluec*
finger	*dei, doi, doit*	full	*plain, plein, ses*
fire	*feu, fou*	full of fervor	*balt*
first	*premiers, primes*	full of joy	*joieus*
fled	*fuit*	furious	*enragié, iré, irié*
flee from	*fuier, fuir*	furnishing	*garnis*
flesh	*char, charn*	further	*avant, mais*
flower	*flor, florir*	furthermore	*mes*
fly	*voler*		
folding chair for important person	*faldestoed, faldestuef, faldestuel*		

Word List (English to Old French)

English	Old French	English	Old French
		grant	creanter, durrai, granter, otrei, otrier, otroier

G, g

English	Old French
game	table
garden	vergier
gave	dona, done, doné, duna
Gawain (a name)	gavain, gavains
Gawain's	gawain
generous	riche
gentle	bealz, dolz, dous
gentleman	chevaliers
gifts	dons
girl	polle, pucele
girl of noble birth	damoiselle
give	baillier, comander, doner, rendre
give in	concreidre
given	doner
glad	lies, liés
gladly	volentiers
glanced-at	regarda
glorious	glorious
glory	gloire
glove	gant
go	ala, aler, alés, alez, en, met, venir, vois
go away	se departir
go by	trespasser
go out	issir
go to the help of	secorer
god	deu, element
god's	deu
godson	filuel
goes	vait, vet
going	alé, alés
gold	or
gone	alé, alés, alez
good	ben, biaus, bien, bon, bone, bons
good fortune	ben, bien
grace	clementiam, merci, pardon
grand	granz
grandson	neveu, nevot
granted	otroié
grass	erbre
great	grans, grant, magne
greatly	durement, forment, grant
greay	grant
Greek (a name)	gré, gri, grieu, griu
green	verde, vert
greet	salu, saluer
greeted	salua
greeting	s'entrefirent
greyhounds	levriers
grief	dol, duel, ennui
gripped	estraint
grow	creistre, croistre
grow worse	angregier
guard	garder, gardés, guardent
guarded	guarderent

H, h

English	Old French
ha	ha
had	a, aveit, avoit, deüst, est, fait, fet, firent, fist, fu, furent, fust, la, lait, l'aveit, l'avoient, l'avoit, l'orent, orent, ot, sa, tel, tindrent
had-been	esté, fusse
had-he	a
had-not	n'avoit
had-they	orent
hair	cheveleüre
hall	sale
hand	main
handsome	beals, bel, gent
hang	pendre
hanged	pendre
hanging	pendus
happen	avenir
happened	avenu, avenue, avint, fu, issi

82

Word List (English to Old French)

English	Old French	English	Old French
happy	balt, lié, lies, liés, liet, liez	he-did	s'en
harbour	havene, port	he-did-not-have	n'avoit
hard	dur, durement, fort	he-embraced	l'acola
harm	damage, foler, laid, mal, mesfacent, tucha	he-for	k'il
		he-had	aveit, avoit, furent
harmed	damage	he-her	l'a
harried	hasta	he-him	l'en
has	a, avra, est, il, l'ait, tel	he-is	s'est
has-done	fait	held	tenoit, tens, tint
has-it	fist	he-left	laissa
haste	hasté	hell	enfern
hasten	se hasteier, se haster	hello	ha
hated	haï	he-looked	regarde
hate-him	haïst	he-loved	ama, enamé
hates	het	help	socors, sucurs
hatred	haine	he-perceived	s'aparceit
hauberk	halberc, osberc	her	la, l'a, le, l'en, les, li, l'i, lui, sis, son, sun
haughty	enorgoillir	here	ça, çai, chi, ci, ici, issi, l'en
have	ai, as, auroit, aveir, avés, avoir, avrez, faites, l'ai, tenir	her-had	l'aveit
		her-married	lespousa
have back	ravoir	her-own	sa
have to	devoir	he-runs	curut
have-I	ai	he-stayed	herberja
have-I-loved	namai	he-stopped	s'aresta
have-we	avum	he-took	mené
he	a, ce, celui, cil, el, ele, en, est, fu, hum, i, il, l'a, le, l'en, les, li, lors, lui, mes, ne, quis, se, s'en, ses, s'est	he-wanted	volentiers
		he-wanted-to	voloit
		he-was	est, esteit, le, li, s'est
		he-went	ala, alout
		he-wished	volenté, voloit
he, him	lui	hidden	celé, muciés, tapis
head	chief, teste	hide	celes
health	santé	high	alt, altain, aut, halt, haut
hear	entendre, odir, oëz, oir, oïr	hill	pui
heard	antendu, conterent, entendu, l'oïrent, lot, oï, orent	him	cil, et, hum, il, ki, l'a, le, l'en, li, l'i, lui, mi, se, sel, si
heart	coer, cor, cors, cuer, curage	him-had	l'aveit
heath	lande	him-loved	l'amerent, l'amout
heathen	pagien, paien	himself	meïsmes, seul
heaven	ciel	him-there	l'en
he-called	apela	him-they-would-love	lameront
he-came-to	l'uis		

Word List (English to Old French)

English	Old French	English	Old French
his	*la, l'a, le, les, li, lor, sa, se, ses, si, soens, son, sun*	if-some	*s'alcune*
		ignorance	*nonsavoir*
		i-hear	*oï*
his-adventure	*s'aventure*	i-implore-you	*plorés*
his-shoulder	*l'espaule*	i-know	*sai*
hit	*fiere*	ill	*enferm, mal*
hither	*ça, çai*	illness	*enfermeté, mal*
hoisted	*sachierent*	illuminated	*alumer*
hold	*tenir*	I-may	*puisse*
hollow	*cruese*	immediately	*endreit, maintenant, sempre, sempres, tantost, tost*
holy	*saint*		
home	*maisun*		
homes	*maisun*		
honor	*anor, enor, fei, foi, honestét, onor*	important	*alt, aut, halt*
		in	*a, ad, al, as, el, en, ens, sun*
honored	*honore*	in front of	*devant*
honour	*honor, honors*	in here	*ceanz, seans*
horn	*cor, corn*	in order that	*com, cum*
horror	*poür, tristece*	in the direction of	*de vers, devers*
horses	*ceval*	in the middle	*par mi, parmi*
hounds	*chiens*	in the midst of	*entre*
hour	*eure, ore*	in the presence of	*devant*
house	*maison, maisun, ostel*	in vain	*mar*
household	*maisnie, maisniee*	in-accord	*acorda*
how	*coment, comment, cum, sa*	in-choice	*anchois*
		in-days-passed	*jadis*
how-to	*comment*	indeed	*ja, voir*
hunger	*faim*	indicate	*demostrer*
hunt	*chacier, chasser*	indicated	*enseigna*
hunters	*veneür*	inform	*enseignier*
hunting	*chace*	in-front	*devant*
huntsmen	*veneor*	ingenuity	*engien*
hurry	*espleitiez*	inquired	*enquis*
husband	*seignur, sire*	inside	*dedenz, ens*
		in-such-way	*cumfaitement*
		intensely	*merveille*
		intention	*maniere*

I, i

English	Old French	English	Old French
		in-the-middle	*enmi*
		in-those	*es*
i	*i, ja, j'ai, je, jel, jeo, jes, jeu, jo, jol, jou, me*	into	*en*
		in-trouble	*malbaillis*
		invent	*engeignier, engignier*
i-am	*sui*	inventory	*livre*
i-begin	*m'entremet*	invoke	*reclamer*
if	*se, s'en, si*	I-pray	*pri*
if-he	*S'il*	Ireland (a place)	*d'yrlande, Yrlande*
if-him	*s'il*		
if-she	*s'el*		

Word List (English to Old French)

English	*Old French*	English	*Old French*
iron	*fer*	killed	*mort, ocioient, ocis, ocit, tué*
is	*a, as, en, est, fu, i, la, m'est, s'est*	kinf	*roi*
I-see	*voi!*	king	*lui, regem, rei, reis, roi, rois, rois*
I-shall-become	*devenrai*	kingdom	*regne*
I-shall-bring	*aporterai*	kings	*roi*
I-shall-not-be	*nestoie*	king's	*rei, roi*
is-humbled	*s'umilie*	kiss	*baisier*
island	*ille, isle*	kissed	*baisa, baisie*
is-not	*n'ait*	kisses	*baise*
it	*a, ce, ceo, ceu, ço, il, la, le, li, s'en*	kneeling	*s'agenoilla*
it-is	*c'est, est*	knew	*sachiés, saveit, savoient, savoit, set, seümes, sot, sout, vis*
its	*el*		
it-seems	*esciënt*	knight	*bacheler, chevalier, chevaliers*
it-took-away	*lenporta*		
it-was	*estoit*	knights	*chevalerie, chevaliers*
i-understand	*j'entent*	knock down	*abatre*
ivory horn	*olifant*	know	*apercevoir, sachiés, savez, savoir*
i-want	*vueil*		
I-will	*jel*	knowing	*saveit, set*
i-will-eat	*mangerai*	knowledge	*esciënt*
i-will-give	*donrai*	known	*cuneüz, seü*
I-will-show	*mosterroie*	known-him	*veü*
i-wish	*vueil, vus*	knows	*set*
I-would-be	*sereie*	know-you	*sachiés*

J, j

jest	*gab*		
Jesus (a name)	*jesu*		
joy	*joi, joie*		
joyed	*joians*		
joyful	*joians, lié, liet*		
joyous	*joius*		
just	*comment, or*		

K, k

L, l

keep	*tenir*	lace	*las*
keep from	*astenir*	lady	*dame*
kept	*gardoient*	laid-up	*colchié*
kill	*morir, ocire*	laid-waste	*degasté*
		lament	*se dementer*
		land	*lande, païs, terre*
		lands	*terres*
		large	*grans, grant*
		largesse	*largece*
		laughed	*riant*
		lay	*jut, lais*
		lay siege	*asseoir*
		lays	*lais*
		lead	*deduire, mener*
		leagues	*lieues*
		leaping	*lança*

Word List (English to Old French)

English	*Old French*	English	*Old French*
leapt	*sailli*	looked-at	*regarda, regardé*
leave	*congié, cungié, guerpir, lais, laissier, partir, se departir*	looked-upon	*regardé*
		loot	*eschec*
		lord	*dam, dan, seignor, seignur*
led-himself	*cunteneit*	lose	*perdre*
left	*issus, laissa, laissier*	loss	*perdre*
leg	*jambe*	lost	*perdeit, perdi, perdu, perduz*
legitimate	*leal, loial*		
lend	*prester*	love	*amer, amor, chier, eim, s'amur*
less	*mains, meins, moins*		
lesson	*moralité*	loved	*amé, amee, amer, amez, amot, chier*
let	*fai, laissier, les, lur*		
let-be	*lairés, laissast, soit*	lover	*amant*
letter	*chartre*	lowered	*baissié*
let-us	*alum, laissons*	loyal	*leal, loial*
let-us-leave	*laissuns*	lying	*gisant*
liberal art	*art*		
lie	*favele, gesir, mentir*		
lie down	*couchier, se coucher*		
liege	*liges*		
life	*estre, metra, vie*		
lift up	*lever*		
light	*legier, ligier, loigier*		
light-hearted	*legier, ligier, loigier*		
likewise	*aussi*		
lily	*lil*		
lineage	*lignage*		
listen	*entendés, entent, escouta, oëz*		
listen to	*escolter*		
little	*pau, petit, poi, pou*		
live	*deduire, vie, vif*		
lived	*maneit*		
loaded	*charga*		
lodge	*herbergier*		
lodging	*l'ostel, l'ostel*		
long	*loing, lonc, long, longement, lung, lungement*		
long-after	*lungement*		
look	*esgardés, veés*		
look at	*aviser*		
look for	*quere, querre*		
look-at	*esguardez*		
look-at-him	*regarder*		
looked	*regardé*		

M, m

English	*Old French*
madam	*dame*
made	*faire, faiseit, fait, firent, sont*
made-known	*coneü*
maiden	*pucele, pucelë*
maidens	*puceles*
make	*faire, faites*
make a mistake	*mesprendre*
make known	*reveler*
makes	*faites*
man	*hom, home, huem, hume, ome*
manifest	*apert*
manner	*guise*
mannered	*samblant*
mantle	*mantel*
many	*asez, assés, bien, maint, meinte, menoit, molt, mout, mult, plenté, pluisors, plusur, plusurs, sovent*
many a	*maint*
mariners	*mariniers, maronier*
married	*espusee*
marry	*esposer*

Word List (English to Old French)

English	Old French	English	Old French
marvel	merveille, merveillié, merveillier	most	mult, plus
		mother	mere
marvellously	merveille	mound	tertre
marvels	merveilles	mountain	mont, montaigne, pui
mass	masse	mountains	montaignes
matter	afaire, chaloir	mounted	monta, monte, monté, montee
matting	nate		
may	poés, porras	mourn	plaindre
me	ja, jo, me, mei, mes, moi	mouth	bouche, buche
		much	asez, assés, bien, est, guaires, molt, mout, mult, tel, tres
meal	mangier		
mean	mal		
meat	char, charn	must	dois
meet	assanler, assembler, encontrer	mutated	mua
		my	ma, mes, mon, mun
meeting	parlement	my-hand	manel
Melion (a name)	Melïon, Melïons	my-heart	cuer
melody	chant	my-lord	sire
memory	memoire	my-lords	segnor
men	homes, humes	my-love	m'amur
menace	manace, menace	myself	meïsmes
mercy	merci		
message	mes, message	# N, n	
messenger	message		
might	meute, vertu	naked	nu, nus
mile	liue, live	name	nom, nomer, non
mine	me, mei, moi	naught	ne
mine-is	m'est	near	lez
miracle	miracle	neck	col
misdeed	mesfaire	neighbours	veisins
miserable	chaitif	nephew	neveu, nevot
misery	poverté	nets	rois, rois
misfortune	pechié	never	ja, jamais, ne, n'i, nonque, onques, unc, unkes
misguided	meserrez		
mislead	deçoivre		
missed	perdeit	nevertheless	nekedent
mistake	colpe, cope, corpe, pechié, tort	never-will	n'i
		next to	dales, dalles
mistreatment	mesfait	next to; beside	delé, deleiz, deles
mistress	drue	next-to	joste, s'alout
money	argent	night	nuis, nuit
monk	moine, monie	night-fall	anuita
more	mais, mes, plus, plusur, remest	no	ne, nul, nule
		noble	debonaire, esteit, gentil, prous
more-than	plus		
morning	main	nobly	noblement

Word List (English to Old French)

English	Old French	English	Old French
noise	estor, estorm, vois, voiz	of whom	dont, dunt
no-longer	ne	of-a	d'un
none	ne, nel, n'i, nul, nuls	of-a-man	d'ome, d'ume
none-at-all	mie	of-arms	d'armes
no-one	ne, N'i	of-ermine	dermine
nor	ne, nel, n'en, ni	off	a
Normans (a name)	Norman	offer	presenter
nor-meet	n'encontre	of-him	l'ai, qu'um
nose	nes	of-Ireland	dyrlande, d'yrlande
noselessly	esnasees	of-it	en
noses	nes	of-men	d'ommes
not	enne, mie, ne, nel, nen, n'en, nes, n'i, non, nul, nule, pas	of-one	d'une, l'une
		often	sovent
		of-the	ala, del, des
not any	nul	of-them	des, en, eüs, l'en, li
not at all	nïent	of-this	del
not-at-all	mie	of-took	demené
not-had	n'out	of-where	dont
not-has	n'a	of-whom	dont
not-has-been	n'a	old	veil, vieil, viez
not-having	n'a, n'avoit	on	a, ad, en, ens, seur, sor, soure, sur
nothing	feiz, nel, nïent, rien, rien?	on top of	en
notice	apercevoir	once	onques
noticed	l'aperceut, ravisa, ravisé	one	c'uns, i, icel, le, om, on, un, une, uns
not-is	n'est	only	deseure, ne, seul, soelent
not-of	n'en	on-which	en
now	adont, ja, jai, or, ore, orent	open	apert
		oppose	contredire
now-is-the-end	explicit	opposition	cuntredit
nude	nuz	or	ne, o, ou, u
		orchard	vergier

O, o

English	Old French	English	Old French
		order	comander, rover
		ordered	mandez, rova
oars	aviron	origin	parage
oath	sairement	or-other	n'autre
observe	viseter	other	altre, autre
octave	huitaves	our	nostre
of	a, al, ala, de, del, des, e, en, ki, la, on, ot, se	out	fors, hors
		out of	hors
of it	en	out-of	de
of noble lineage	emparenté	outside	fors
of the king	regal	out-stretched	tendre
of which	dont, dunt	over	seur, sor, soure, sur

Word List (English to Old French)

English	*Old French*
overcome	*veintre*
overcome completely	*tresprendre*
overload	*encombrer*
owe	*dei*
own	*baillier, demeine*
oxen	*bues*

P, p

English	*Old French*
pagan	*pagien, paien*
page	*bacheler, bachelor*
pain	*dolor, dolur, enoi, enui*
palace	*palais*
palfrey	*palefroi*
pardon	*pardoner*
parent	*parent*
part	*part, partez, piece*
parts	*pars*
part-with	*partir*
party	*feste*
pass	*trespasser*
passed	*pas*
path	*chemin, sentier*
pay	*prist*
pay attention	*entendre, penser*
pay attention to	*escolter*
peace	*pes*
peace-treaty	*pais*
peasant	*païsant*
people	*gent, suens*
period	*terme*
period of time	*terme, termine*
perish	*perdre, perir*
permission	*congié, pardon*
permission to leave	*congié*
persecution	*empedement*
person	*figure, ren, rien*
persuaded	*losenga*
petite	*petite*
physical or moral weakness	*enfermeté*
picked-up	*relevee*
piece	*piece*
piece-of-bread	*pain*
piece-of-meat	*lardé*
pigeon	*colomb, colon*
pine tree	*pin*
pity	*merci, pitié*
place	*asseoir, lieu, meterés, metez, place*
places	*lieus*
plain	*plaigne*
plates	*dobliers*
play	*joer*
please	*plaire*
pleased	*bel, lié*
pleasure	*deduit*
plenty	*plenté*
plunder	*preie*
point out	*enseignier*
politely	*belement*
poor	*povre*
port	*port*
portion	*part*
poverty	*poverté*
power	*vertu*
powerful	*riche*
praise	*loër*
praised	*loer, losenja, proisie*
pray	*orer, preier, pri, prier*
prayed	*orent*
prayer	*oraison, orison, priement*
precious cloth	*paile*
precious object	*parament*
precisely	*endreit*
prepare	*atorner, atornés*
prepared	*apareillié, apareillier*
preparing	*fu*
present	*porofrir, present, presenter*
presented	*presentee*
presently	*ore*
pretense	*feintise*
previously	*suliëz*
prison	*piere, pierre, prison, serre*
privately	*priveement*
prize	*pris*
proceed	*aler*

Word List (English to Old French)

English	*Old French*	English	*Old French*
proclaim	*clamer*	really	*bien, voirement*
profession	*menestier*	realm	*roiauté*
promise	*acreanter, fiance*	reason	*entente, raison, raisun*
proper	*droit*	receive	*baillier*
prosecute	*asproier*	receive as guest	*herbergier*
protect	*gaitier*	received	*prent, receüe*
protection	*garant, garent*	receives	*prent*
protrude	*empeindre*	recognised	*con, coneü, coneüs, conut, ravisa, reconeüs*
proud	*fier*		
prowess	*proece*		
pull	*tirer*	recognize	*aviser, reconoistre*
pure	*mer, mier*	recommend	*comander*
purposed	*purpensa*	recounted	*aconté, conté, contee, cunta, cunté*
pursue	*porchacier*		
pursued	*conseü*	recovery	*reconfort*
purveyor	*porveor*	re-dress	*reveste*
put	*feiz, mectre, met, metre, mettre*	refined	*cointe*
		refuse	*veer*
puts	*met*	refuse to believe	*mescroire*
		regain	*ataindre*

Q, q

		regret	*dolans, plaindre*
		reject	*geter, giter*
queen	*raine, reine, roine, roïne*	rejoice	*esleecier*
		rejoiced	*joie*
queried	*enquis*	rejoicing	*joie, sesjoï*
questioned	*mise*	relate	*conter*
questions	*demanda*	released	*descuplé*
quickly	*hastivement, menu, menut, tost*	relieved	*guarie*
		remain	*demorer, ester, maindre, remanoir*
quilts	*kieutes*		
quiver	*bercerië*	remained	*remest, remez*
		remains	*relef*

R, r

		remedy	*resort*
		remember	*resovenir*
		rememberance	*remembrance*
race	*gent*	remove-boots	*deschaucier*
rage	*rage*	removed	*osta*
ran	*corus, curut*	removed-boots	*descaucha*
rank	*parage*	repair	*refaire*
rather	*ainc, ains, ainz, assez, mais, mels, miels*	repeated	*recorderent*
		repeatedly	*suventes*
ravaged	*escilloit*	resign	*conserrer, consirrer*
reach	*ataindre*	resist	*contredire, remanoir*
ready	*apresté*	respect	*anor, enor, onor*
real	*verai*	responded	*respont, respunt*

Word List (English to Old French)

English	*Old French*	English	*Old French*
rest	*reposer, se reposer*	sad	*dolans, mat*
restriction	*resort*	sadness	*tristece*
retained	*retenu*	said	*dïent, dïent, dist, dit, fait, fet*
retain-him	*retenir*		
retinue	*conroi, conrois*	sail	*eskiper*
retire	*colchier*	sailing	*siglant*
return	*rendre, retor, retorn, revienc, torner*	sails	*voiles*
		salute	*saluer*
returned	*atorna, rendi, rendu, repaira, repairiez, retorna, retornee, retornés, tornee, turnez*	sat	*sisent*
		savage	*salvage*
		saw	*choisi, veïst, veü, veüe, veüs, vindrent, virent, vit, voit*
reveal	*reveler*	say	*di, dire*
revealed	*descovri*	saying	*dist*
revolt	*reveler*	says	*dis*
reward	*guerredoner*	scraps	*relef*
rich	*riche, riches*	se	*ves*
riches	*argent*	sea	*marine, mer*
richly	*richement*	seated	*assis, l'assist*
rich-silk	*samit*	secretly	*coiement*
ride	*chevauchie*	seduce	*engeignier, engignier, enorter*
right	*droit, endreit*		
ring	*anel*	see	*aviser, veés, veïr, veoir*
risen	*levé*		
risked	*aventure*	seek	*porchacier*
rivers	*riviere*	seen	*veü, vit*
road	*veie*	sees	*veit*
roamed	*erré*	segment	*piece*
robe	*giron*	seize	*prendre, tenir*
rode	*iront*	seized	*pris, prist*
Romans (a name)	*romains*	sense	*sen, sens*
room	*chambre*	sent-for	*manda, mandee*
rooms	*chambres*	separate	*oster*
rose	*leva, rose*	servant	*pucele, servant, vallet*
round	*reont*	servants	*sergant*
royal	*regal*	serve	*servir*
royal apartment	*chambre*	served	*servi, servir, servoient*
ruin	*eissil, essil, issil*	service	*menestier, servise*
ruined	*agastis*	set	*mis, mise*
ruled	*regnoit*	set up	*asseoir*
run	*corre*	seven	*set*
running	*corant, curut, fuiant*	several	*pluisor, plusor*
		sewn	*cosu*
		shall-have	*l'avras*

S, s

Word List (English to Old French)

English	Old French	English	Old French
shall-I	n'avrai	sleeping	dormant
shall-I-love	amerai	slept	culchier
shall-lie	mentirai	small	petit
shall-not	ne	smash to pieces	pecier
shall-stop	lairai	smell	sentir
shall-touch	toucherai	snatched	esracha
shame	honte, hunte	so	ce, dunc, fu, issi, si, tant, vis
shamed	honte	so much	tant
shaped	mollee	so-as-this	ensi
she	el, ele, est, i, l'a, le, li, se, ses	somber	have
shed tears	plorer	some	alkun, alqant, aucun
she-dressed	s'apareillot	somebody	alme, ame, anme, arme
she-has	la	somehow	coment
shelter	herbergier	somewhat	alques
she-sent-for	l'enveia	so-much	tant
she-was-terrified	s'esfrea	son	fil, filuel
shield	escu	song	chant
shields	escus	son-of	fiex
ship	nef	sons	fiex
shore	gravoi	soon	maintenant, ore, orent, tost
shortly	briement	soon-as	tost
should	devez, doit	sorely	durement
shoulders	col, espauleüre	sorrow	dolans
shout	braire, crier, escrier	sorrowful	dolent
shouted	escrié	sought-for	demandez
show	demostrer, mener	soul	alme, ame, anima, anme, arme
showed	mostra	sound	soner, suner
shy away	feindre	sparlking	rians
sick	have	speak	parler
side	costé	speech	oraison, orison, parler, parole, raison
sides	parz	spin	filer
sight	ses	spiritual purity	virginitét
silver	argent	splendid	riche, riches
simple bed	grabatum	splendour	richoise
sin	colpe, cope, corpe, pechié	spoke	parla
since	puis	spoken	parlé
sing	braire, chanter	spoke-to	parla
single	seus	squire	escuier, escuiers
sir	dam, dan	stag	cerf
sire	sire	stage	commencement
sires	seignur	staircase	degré
sit	seoir		
skill	engien, engin		
sleep	som, some		

Word List (English to Old French)

English	*Old French*	English	*Old French*
stake	ré, rei, rez	sure	seur, sur
stand	ester, estut	surprised	esbai
standard bearer	gunfanuner	surrounded	avironé, environ
standing	estait, estant	suspect	mescroire
stars	estoiles	sustain	sostenir
start	comencier	sweet	debonaire, dolz, dous, dulz
stay	demoree, demorer, maindre, remanoir	swift	hastif
stayed	esteit	swoon	se pasmer
steered	corent	sword	espee
steersman	esturmans	swords	espees
steward	senescal		
stick	baston, verge		
sticks	gamais		
still	encor, encore, uncore		
stirrup	estrié, estrier		

T, t

English	*Old French*
table	table
take	mener, menrés, prendre
take hold of	prendre
take off	tolir
take-back	reprendre
take-care	guardez
taken	mena, menés
taken-aside	prise
taken-away	enmena, toli
takes	meine
talk	parler
tall	grant
tame	privés
task	servise
teach	enseignier
tear	deciré
teeth	denz
tell	di, dirai, dire, dis, dist, dites, noncier
tells	direit
temple	temple
ten	x
tenderly	tendrement
term	terme
territory	chambre
than	de, que
thanked	mercïé
thanks	mercie
than-worn	n'afubla

English	*Old French*
stomach	pance
stone	piere, pierre
stones	pieres
stood	leva
stop	fenir, finir
stopped	arestus
stopping	arestés
story	favele
straight	dreit, droit
strangled	estrangla
street	rue
strength	vertu
stretched-out	portendus
strife	estris
striving	travailliez
strong	alt, aut, corsus, fier, fort, halt, riche
struck	feru
study	estude, estudie
subsequently	end, ent, puis
such	cele, ceo, si, tant, tel
such-time	tant
suffer	pener
suffered	traveillié
suffering	dol, dolor, duel, paine, peine, penés
summon	apeler
supple	legier, ligier, loigier
supplied	garnie
support	sostenir

93

Word List (English to Old French)

English	*Old French*	English	*Old French*
that	a, ce, cel, cele, ceo, ceu, cil, ço, e, est, ki, k'il, la, l'a, qu'a, que, qui, qu'il, tant	the-nets	rois
		the-next-day	l'ajornee
		the-one	cil
		the-other	l'altre, l'autre
that much	si	the-palace	palais
that way	si	the-port	port
that-Arthur	c'artus	there	i, il, ilec, iluec, iluoc, la, l'en, vet
that-day	jur		
that-he	k'il		
that-heard	l'oï	the-recounting	conte
that-in	qu'en	therefore	donc, kar, pur
that-one	celui	there-were	estoient
that-she	qu'ele	there-will-be	sera
that-time	cele	the-ring	l'anel
the	a, al, as, cel, cele, ces, cis, de, el, la, le, les, li, ses	the-same	itel
		these	cez
		the-shield	l'escu
the-adventure	l'aventure	the-ship	nef
the-article	lart	the-skies	ciel
the-beast	beste	the-squire	lescuier, l'escuier
the-clothing	despueille	the-story	L'aventure
the-country	païs	the-table	dois
the-devil	deables	the-time	piece
the-end	chief	the-trappings	conroi
the-event	l'aventure	the-truth	verité
the-feet	piés	the-weather	tans
the-forest	bois	the-wife	femme
theft	ravine	the-will-be	seront
the-harbour	port	the-wind	vens
the-hunt	chacier	the-woods	boscage
their	leur, lor, lur	they	cil, i, il, le, les, li, l'ont, l'unt, on, ont, se, s'en, s'i, sont, sunt, unt
the-keep	doignon		
the-king	rei, roi, rois		
the-kingdom	roialme	they-call	l'apelent
the-knight	chevalier	they-came	vienent
the-land	païs	they-did	font
the-last	cist	they-find	truevent
them	en, les, lor	they-had	avoient, dont, eüz
the-man	home	they-hated	enhaïrent
the-meal	mangier	they-live	viveient
the-meat	lardé	they-said	dïent
the-morning	demain, l'endemain	they-saw	virent, voient
then	a, donc, dont, en, lait, lors, puis, que, s'en, si, unt	they-say	dïent
		they-served	servoient
		they-speak	parleront
		they-went	issirent, vindrent
the-name	nun	they-were	estoient, furent, sunt

Word List (English to Old French)

English	Old French	English	Old French
they-were-making	faisoient	together	comunalment, ensamble, ensemble
they-would-have	l'eüssent		
thick	espés	together with	ensemble od
thing	chose, cose, ren, rien	to-get-up	redrecier
things	cose	to-go	aler, errer
think	cuidier, penser	to-greet	contre
thirty	trente	to-help	aidier
thirty four	trente et quatre	to-him	ariere, li
this	a, ce, cel, cele, ceo, cest, ceste, ceu, cil, cis, cist, ço, est, euc, ice, iceste, l'a, le, les, li, o, ou, sa, si	to-him-they	l'ont
		to-leave	laissier
		to-lie	gesir, gisir
		to-lose	perduz
		to-love	amer
		to-make	faire
this-day	hui	to-me	cha!, me, mei, m'en, moi, mun
this-he	cil		
this-they	l'ont		
those	celes, cels	tonight	anuit
thought	quidot, tient	too much	trop
thought-they	quidouent	took	demena, demené, mena, mené, menés, menez, pris, prist, toluz
thousand	millier		
threatened	manaça, manacié		
three	iii, trei, treis, trois		
threw	geté	to-part	partir
throne	faldestoed, faldestuef, faldestuel	torches	chierges
		to-recount	cunter
through	par, par mi, parmi	torment	asproier, enoi, enui, paine, peine
throw	geter, giter		
thus	adont, ça, issi, si, s'i	torn-to-pieces	lardoir
time	eure, feiz, ore, piece, tans, tens, veiz	torture	pener
		to-seek	querre
times	feiz, fois	to-seize	saisir
time-to-time	sovent	to-separate	desevrer
tired	lassés, traveilliés	to-sleep	dormir
title	nom, non	to-speak	parla
to	a, ad, al, de, del, en, encontre, ert, se, seur, sor, soure, sur, vers	to-take	mener
		to-talk-with	parler
		totally	tuz
		to-the	al, ax, la
to-ask	demandasse	to-the-ground	gravier
to-be	seit	to-touch	touchier
to-bear	porter	touch	toucerés, touchiés
to-bite	mordre	touched	toucha, touchié, touciés
to-bring	anemis		
to-catch	prandre	touched-him	touchast
today	oi, ue, ui	touches	touchiés
to-do	desfaire, face, faire	tourney	tornoier
to-embrace	enbracier	toward	vers

Word List (English to Old French)

English	Old French	English	Old French
towards	contre, encontre, envers, vers	unnatural	desnaturés
		unrefined	dur
tower	tor	until	desi, tant, tresqu', trusqu'
town	cit, citet		
to-you	vos	until now	ça en arriere
trace	trace	unto	en
travelled	tint	up	amont, sus, suz
travels	tint	up to	a, ad, jusqu'a, tresqu', trusqu'
treated	bailliz, mis		
tree	bois, bos	upon	sor
tremble	trembler	urge	enorter
trick	engingnier	us	nus
tricked	engané, engignié	used	suleit
troops	compaigne	utter	geter, giter, soner, suner
trouble	damage, guerre		
troubled	esbai, pesa		
true	verai		
true	veraie	## V, v	
true	veritez		
true	voir	valiant	vaillant
truly	voir	vanquish	veintre
truth	voir	various	divers
try	entendre	veering	venus
tumult	estor, estorm	vermillion	vermeil
turn	atorner, torner	very	durement, forment, grant, molt, mout, mult, tres
turned	tornerent		
turned-away	tornés		
turned-to	torné	very much	forment
twenty	xx	very well	asez, assés
two	doi, dous, ii	very-important	munte
		very-much	molt
## U, u		very-well	assés, bonement, molt, tresbien
		village	rue
		virgin	virge
ugly	vilain	visible	aparant, apert
uncle	oncles	visit	viseter
unclothed	despoillié	voice	vois, voiz
under	a, desos, desous, sos, soz, suz	vow	sw, voa
		vows	veu
under-pressed	suzprist		
understand	entendre	## W, w	
understanding	sages		
unhappy	dolans		
unhappy person	entrepris	wait	atendu
unhealthy	enferm	waited	atendi, targa
unleashed	descoplé	wait-for-me	m'atendés

Word List (English to Old French)

English	Old French	English	Old French
waiting	atendi	went-up	monta
wall	mur	wept	plora
want	quere, querre, veus, voloir, vueil, vueille	were	erent, errant, esté, estoit, eüsse, fait, furent, fus, sont
wanted	voleit, volt, vout	werewolf	bisclavret, garulf
wants	volt	wetched	dolent
war	guerre	we-will-see	verruns
war cry	enseigne	what	cument, que, quei, quel, qu'est, qui, qu'il
was	a, avoit, en, ert, est, esté, ester, estoit, fist, fu, fust, li, l'uis, ot, s'en, seroit, s'est, sont	what is surprising	merveille
		what-have	Qu'ai
was-all	tot	what-he	quanque
was-he	esteit, s'en	when	com, comme, qant, quant, que
washed	lava, lavé		
was-it-not-for	fuissent	where	c'on, ou, u
was-made	faisoit	whether	s'il, u
wasteland	dessert	which	dunt, ke, ki, qu'avez, que, quel, qu'en, qui, qu'il
was-to	devoit		
watch	verra		
watch over	garder	which-he	k'il
watched	veü	which-is	qu'est
way	guise, maniere, veie	which-of	qu'il
way of life	estre	which-she	qu'ele
ways	endreit	which-that	qu'il
we	nos, nus	whirl around	tornoier
weak	enferm, vain	white	blanc, blance
weapon	fer	who	ert, ki, le, que, qui, s'en
wear	porter		
wearing	vestu	who-here	qu'ici
weary	pené	who-him	celui
weather	tans, tens	whole	tot
week	semeine	whose	dont, dunt
weeping	plorant, plorer	why	porcoi
weighed-upon	pesa	wide	lee
we-leave	lairomes	wife	espuse, feme, femme
well	assés, bel, bien	wife-his	feme
well-being	ben, bien, santé	wild rose	aiglantier, aiglent
wel-tell	dirons	will	qu'en
went	ala, alé, alés, alez, alout, deci, forvoient, issu, repairié, sont, tint, tostans, va, vait, venoit, venu, vers, vint, vont	will-be	serai
		will-do	ferez
		willed	volt
		will-he-have	avra
		will-hunt	chacerai
		willing	volentiers
went-forwards	tostans	willingly	volentiers
went-to	alés	will-make	fera

Word List (English to Old French)

English	Old French	English	Old French
will-part	*partirai*		
will-tell	*dirai*		
wind	*oré, vent*		
wine	*vin*		
wise	*sages*		
wish	*volenté, voloie*		
wished	*volentés, voloie, voloit, volt, vout*		
wished-to	*voloit*		
wishes	*veu*		
wishing	*voille*		
with	*a, atot, avec, avoc, avoec, avuec, cum, de, en, ensemble, i, mes, o, od, of, ot, qu'el*		
with-a	*d'une*		
without	*sans, senz*		
wolf	*leu, leus*		
wolves	*leu, leus, lous*		
woman	*dame, femme*		
women	*femes, femmes*		
wonder	*merveille*		
wonders	*merveille*		
wood	*bois*		
woods	*bois, boscages*		
word	*faites, mot, parlement, parole, raison, vois, voiz*		
words	*mot*		
world	*mont, mund, secle, seule, siecle*		
worse	*peüst*		
worship	*adurer*		
worthy-man	*prozdum*		
would	*deüst, prendra*		
would-be	*fussent*		
would-go	*venra*		
would-have	*eüsent, eüst, l'eüst*		
would-have-seen	*veïsciés*		
would-look-like	*semblereit*		
would-recount	*contera*		
wrapped	*afublez*		
wretched	*mal*		
wretchedness	*eissil, essil, issil*		
wrong	*mar*		
wrongly	*mar*		

X, x

Y, y

English	Old French
Ydel (a name)	*Ydel*
year	*an*
years	*ans*
yet	*encor, encore, si, uncore*
yield	*ploier*
you	*as, die, jo, ne, te, t'i, tu, vos, vus*
you-have	*vus*
you-he	*t'a*
you-heard	*oïe*
young knight aspirant	*bacheler, bachelor*
young man	*bacheler, bachelor*
your	*ta, tes, ton, vo, vos, vostre, voz, vus*
yours	*vus*
you-see	*vei*
you-will	*tu*
Yrien (a name)	*Yrïen*
Yvain's	*l'iwain*

Z, z

English	Old French
zeal	*estude, estudie*

www.ingramcontent.com/pod-product-compliance
Lightning Source LLC
Chambersburg PA
CBHW051420070526
44584CB00023B/3507